THE IDEA
OF
IDENTIFICATION

Gary C. Woodward

State University of New York Press

Published by
State University of New York Press, Albany

For information, address State University of New York Press,
90 State Street, Suite 700, Albany, NY 12207

Production by Judith Block
Marketing by Jennifer Giovani

Library of Congress Cataloging-in-Publication Data

Woodward, Gary C.
    The idea of identification / Gary C. Woodward.
        p. cm. — (SUNY series in communication studies)
    Includes bibliographical references and index.
    ISBN 0-7914-5819-9 (alk. paper) — ISBN 0-7914-5820-2
(pbk. : alk. paper)
        1. Self—Social aspects.   2. Identification.   3. Identity
(Philosophical concept) 4. Social interaction.   I. Title.   II. Series.

BF697.5.S65W66 2003
302'.1—dc21   2002044797
                    10 9 8 7 6 5 4 3 2 1

To
Dean and Diane

CONTENTS

Preface   ix

1   Origins of an Idea   1

2   Conceptualizing Identification: Extensions of a
Burkean View   21

3   Identification, Celebrity, and the Hollywood Film   45

4   Serenades to the Resistant: Successful Uses of
Identification   71

5   Misidentification and Its Sources   97

6   Identification and Commitment in Civic Culture   121

Notes   147

Index   171

PREFACE

As the umbrella term for the sensation of shared experience, "identification" encompasses a physiology, a psychology, and a strong social dimension. The intellectual history of the term is perhaps most closely associated with Sigmund Freud. But the generative ideas for this book follow a different thread that originates most compellingly in the work of the literary and rhetorical critic, Kenneth Burke. Even though Freud was among the many influences on Burke, the principle starting point here is not the evolution and construction of the self. It is, instead, in the aesthetic and socio-rhetorical processes of identification: processes that play out in transient messages that have fleetingly captured a sense of common understanding. In place of the program of psychology, which tends to focus on who we "are" or wish to be, the essential realm of communication is on the construction of meaning that places us inside a larger community. Where the psychology of the self is measured in phases that unfold over a lifetime, communication is more transitory and unstable: more clearly "in the moment."

To be sure, the line that separates rhetorical and aesthetic uses of identification from the psychological is a thin and illusive one, as imprecise as the threshold that divides identification from identity. There are times when the view is improved by crossing over these vague boundaries to get a different perspective from the other side. But there are no simple theoretical or methodological solutions to the challenging conceptual problems related to the assessment of rhetorical effects. Meaning generated through discourse is subjective rather than uniform. It must be *interpreted* through the filter of one's biography rather than *measured* in electrochemical processes of thought. Our biology gives us wonderful equipment with which to establish awareness and significance. And we have learned a good deal about where sensory, memory, and associational functions occur within the brain. But meaning itself is not fully understandable only in terms of physical or behavioral codes.

Hence, the analyst of identification must try to understand a reaction that is sometimes easier to *feel* than explain. We can easily see the outward forms of identification in images and language, but we can only estimate their significance to others. There are times where descriptive language fails us: where words alone are not up to the task of taking us back to where we know we have been.

Even with these significant conceptual problems, the study of identification offers many compensating opportunities. Among the most important is the chance to study how messages gain saliency by building on the energy of another person's experiences. At the very core of communication as a humanistic study is a sense of anticipation about instances of fluency that can be transformative in their impact on audiences. In poetry or film these moments may be found in the perfectly constructed image. In music, the connection might emerge in a familiar passage that is anticipated and reheard with pleasure. Even the rhetoric of public life offers its own rewards. Like the stylus that finds its way into the grooves of an old and familiar record, the words of advocates can sometimes replay memories of an experience that represent the essence of what an audience believes or feels.

Identification is thus a cherished effect of communication: a rhetorical form of superconductivity that permits a total transfer of emotional energy from one being to another. At the heart of our fascination for the theater, the novel, political advocacy, and the representational arts generally, is an unquenchable pleasure in the emotional arcadias these messages can produce. To borrow a phrase from the composer Aaron Copland, a message—in words, images or music—"exteriorizes inner feelings," making them accessible to others.[1]

These moments of lucidity—and sometimes even the missed opportunities for identification—are intrinsically interesting to study. If there is a general lesson to be offered in these pages, it is that identification is both a more primitive and a more varied process than one might first suppose. In our casual usage of the term, we often observe that identification is the product of various forms of similarity, for instance: ideological ("I agree"), demographic ("We are both women"), or shared circumstances ("Both of us grew up on farms"). What more intensive study reveals, however, is our remarkable capacity to extend our empathy to people and situations that have no obvious analogues in our own experience. If we are inclined to do so, we are surprisingly adept at "standing in another person's shoes."

The approach here is deliberately eclectic. While I draw selectively on social and literary theory, social psychology, film criticism, and especially rhetorical theory, this is not a study driven by a single perspective or theoretical system. Role theory and the considerable Burkean canon are this study's primary starting points. They are among various psychological, rhetorical, and aesthetic perspectives outlined in the first three chapters. The case-study approach in the remainder of the book illuminates identification by focusing on specific contexts and details that can account for its creation or destruction.

Equally eclectic is the range of "messages" included here as "discourse." The cases and examples of the book reflect what the reader may consider an unusual collection of expressive and of representational arts, ranging from politics to public sculpture. In these pages there are examples and analyses of personal rhetoric, policy rhetoric, news reports, music, and film narratives. All have the advantage of being transparent in illustrating the identification thread. And all reflect my particular passions, and my intention to recontextualize this concept by moving beyond its traditional psychological and literary roots.

As a state of heightened consciousness, identification transcends disciplinary boundaries even while it serves in its essentially rhetorical function. Indeed, if there can be a general theory of identification, it needs to be enhanced by the cross-fertilization of perspectives that encompass both applied and expressive forms of communication. In these pages, for example, I have noted that film theory has some interesting things to say to rhetorical theorists about the intensity of identifications. Film theorists seem to have identified some subtle variations that literary and rhetorical critics have missed.

I have chosen to explore identification in narrative by looking more at film rather than fiction. Fiction is enormously fertile ground for the construction and destruction of deep affinities. But other scholars have fully explored this landscape. My preference is also for messages and analytical frameworks that speak more to rhetorical rather than literary issues. In these pages, messages are especially worthy of attention if they have succeeded or failed in satisfying the expectations of their audiences.

So in exploring messages that bridge the gaps between people, we are left with a daunting but interesting task. Meaning is not like money; words and images are not universal objects exchanged at fixed rates. Because passions are not easily transferable, identifications can be extremely personal and specific to a moment. But, of course, that is exactly the point. However unique and independent we wish to be, we are also heavily vested in the recurring hope of making lasting connections with others. This book is both an exploration and an appreciation of this very human impulse. Because we have faith in the transformative power of sound, image, and word, we savor the chances they offer of making partners out of strangers.

I am indebted to a number of writers and scholars who have previously illuminated the "dramatistic" and sociorhetorical perspectives reflected in these pages. They include Kenneth Burke, Hugh Dalziel Duncan, Trevor Melia, Joshua Meyrowitz, Richard Sennett, Robert Hughes, Rod Hart, and Erving Goffman. It was an adventure to revisit their scholarship. Thanks are also due to the Sea Shepherd Conservation Society for providing television footage of the Makah whale hunt, the Broad Art Foundation and John Ahearn for permission to reprint an image of a sculpture, and the Roscoe West Library for assistance in locating a number of books and articles.

I owe a special debt to The College of New Jersey and its Faculty Research Committee for providing time to write. Several anonymous reviewers provided by the State University of New York Press offered encouragement and suggestions that significantly strengthened the manuscript. And I am especially grateful to a number of busy colleagues and friends who offered research suggestions or commented on part of the manuscript. They include Shalani Alisharan, David Blake, John Pollock, Jan Robbins, Lois Robbins, Michael Robertson, Susan Ryan, Richard Vatz, Lynn Waterhouse, and Hilary Woodward. Their advice and suggestions significantly improved my work, though the failings that remain are mine alone.

Chapter 1

ORIGINS OF AN IDEA

If we think of identity as a mark of a separate and unified subjectivity, identification is rejection of separateness; it denies the others difference by allowing the subject the excitement of trespass, the thrill of being the other. Art provides us repeated access to such psychic thrills.
> —Elin Diamond, "Rethinking Identification: Kennedy, Freud, Brecht"

You persuade a man only insofar as you can talk his language by speech, gesture, tonality, order image, attitude, idea, identifying your ways with his.
> —Kenneth Burke, *A Rhetoric of Motives*

Identification can be given any one of many characterizations: common ground, inhabiting, projecting, becoming, associating, connecting, and so on. In cinematic terms, identification seems to create a momentary freeze frame: a temporary pause in a world unfolding at twenty-four frames a second. In that short space the brain seems to give us time to take in and absorb a place, a person, or a thought that we already "know." One could alternatively describe identification as the "replay" of a familiar "tape," or the match to a familiar form already in the memory. Whatever the metaphor, we strive to find the right words to account for the extension of identification from its literal Latin root *idem*—meaning "same"—to the much broader but elusive capacity for empathy.

In some ways tracing the intellectual history of so central a human impulse is arbitrary. No single source, faction, or culture can lay claims of exclusivity or discovery to the human tendency toward identification. We have, instead, a long series of complementary and sometimes contradictory systems of thought—ranging from Freud to film theory—which treat the subject as primary to our understanding of how humans establish patterns of significance in their lives. In their finer details these systems agree on very little. But one thing is certain: experience in its many forms leaves its calling card behind, marking specific moments or events as obvious touchstones to our identity. And while we are only at the beginning of a long quest to map the neuroscience of "higher" cognitive processes,[1] we have a long history of interest in identification that spans from ancient rhetorical theory to modern cultural studies.

All of these fields start from the same premise: as individuals we possess a staggering range of symbolic resources that allow us to consider another person's experiences and recognize them as our own. These include the cues of our sensory world—sight, sound, smell, touch—as well as the linguistic tools for communicating these experiences to others. Just in the realm of language, an educated adult may have a vocabulary of forty thousand words, and an intensely verbal person's can reach over one hundred thousand.[2]

We also possess a brain that has an enormous predisposition for visiting and revisiting linkages. Events and feelings accumulated over time strike chords of recognition, providing a consciousness of similarity that is regularized in a kind of "library" of personal rituals. What neuroscience calls "associative learning"[3] builds structures of relationships that may exist as latent thoughts held by our long-term memory, or new thoughts that are a part of our immediate consciousness. Memory obviously gives the brain a significant amount of power to generate associations. Our love of replication, imitation, and ritual keeps many of them close at hand.

Even the impressionistic and abstract products of the arts can trigger a richer range of associations than might seem possible. In physical terms, the image conveyed on the canvas comes to us as light and color measured in angstrom units. Music can be reduced to the sound equivalent of cycles per second, or hertz. But the brain adds much more as associations begin to build up in the memory and are triggered in recall. The cliché that childhood comes with its own "soundtrack" is intuitively true. For nearly all of us memories of adolescence are easily recalled in the context of the popular music of the period. The same principle of association works in other forms of music that carry programmatic associations. For this writer the deliberate rhythmic inflexibility in the last movement of Prokofiev's Fifth Symphony suggests the machine-age modernism of the 20s: a style of rude dominance over the land also captured in the Cubist cityscapes of Joseph Stella and others.[4] I have no idea why I have these identifications, or if they create similar associations with others. But the links are real, and I love the music and images for them.

Music represents an especially tricky category of associations, but it seems strangely well suited to mining the depths of prior experience. At a purely physical or scientific level it may make little sense to attribute to a sequence of *sounds* a meaning that is translated into *visual* terms. But we make such connections all the time. Our senses are constantly feeding us impressions that prompt memories of our past: moments we consciously reconstruct to be better or worse than the original experiences. To be sure, these associations mix the personal and cultural in unpredictable ways. And with its framework of stimulus-response theory, associative learning models hardly seem up to the challenge. Yet it would be a serious underestimation to neglect contexts for identification because they violate narrow and deterministic systems.

The subject of music is relevant in at least one other context. Researchers who study auditory perception note that the pleasure we derive from organized sound flows from more than just the recognition of a familiar tune. Music has, in the words of Robert Jourdain, a "deep structure" that involves an accumulation of expectations learned over time.[5] Certain associations and patterns are held as a kind of common property. Melodies are pleasing or not because they follow certain learned rules in the western twelve-tone scale. The conventions of popular music dictate that where key changes can happen and how a chord progression can be "resolved." Phrases of a song are broken into eight or sixteen bar segments such that a five-bar fragment inserted somewhere in the middle would seem alien. In the words of Aaron Copland, we expect certain rules of "continuity" and "thematic relationships" to be observed, and we are sometimes frustrated when they are not. Considering the works of a member of the German avant-garde, for example, Copland found continual violations of anticipated progressions that were frustrating:

> In this music, one waits to hear what will happen next without the slightest idea of what *will* happen, or why what

happened did happen once it has happened. [Karlheinz] Stockhausen's only chance is to mesmerize the listener. Failing that, one gets bored.[6]

The same is no less true for other forms of discourse. In public rhetoric, the novel, the film, and virtually any representational medium, certain associations and pre-existing forms are held as property. In Kenneth Burke's words, "form is the creation of an appetite in the mind of the auditor, and the adequate satisfying of that appetite."[7]

Form in general is a kind of common property when—as in the case of music—there are rules and conventions to be honored and audience expectations to be met. But form given substance in a particular piece of work is often valued as private property, as when we objectify reproductions of discourse and revisit them for the reliable pleasures they offer. As Evan Eisenberg has noted, there is an unmistakable attraction to the idea of possessing the performances of others.[8] Reproductions of music, films, books and paintings can be purchased and consumed at will. Works that we "own" that have been captured on paper or plastic are part of our world: tokens of specified meaning ready to sustain the routines of our lives.

This preliminary chapter takes a first look at identification by briefly tracing some of the important threads that make up the rhetorical fabric of the rest of the book. These include references to the seminal works of Aristotle, the Sophists, George Herbert Mead, Kenneth Burke, and others, all of whom have contributed related observations about identification and its centrality to the process of communication. The next chapter takes a closer look at the pivotal work of Burke and some of his interpreters.

Caveats and a Preliminary Definition

In exploring the nature of the relationship that momentarily links audience to source, I mean something more than Chaim Perelman's definition that emphasizes "connections and rejections of connections,"[9] but something less elastic than Kenneth Burke's assertion that it includes virtually the entire "function of sociality."[10] The emphasis here is more Western than non-Western, skewed in the direction of single messages or message segments, and more relevant to transactions where the communicator is conscious of an audience beyond the self. Any simple definition of so broad a concept is a potential intellectual tripwire. And there are times in the pages that follow where it will serve the purposes of this study to step outside of the definition offered here. But it is a good starting point to consider identification as *the conscious alignment of oneself with the experiences, ideas, and expressions of others: a heightened awareness that a message or gesture is revisiting a feeling or state of mind we already "know."* Like so many aspects of communication, identification is both a process and an outcome. It includes message-acts offered up for their potential powers of association. And it plays out in audiences by creating predictable and sought-after effects. As such, *identification is experience.*[11] We are usually conscious of its arrival. At its strongest it creates spikes of decisive recognition that can bind us to specific sources, while affirming the boundaries of our own recognized world.

The Rhetorical Frame of Reference

The earliest discussions of rhetorical associations that bind sources and audiences together are usually credited to Aristotle (about 330 B.C.), not because he was literally the first observer of the process, but because, as Burke notes, Aristotle so convincingly places the roots of communication in the impulses of common ground and assimilation. Unlike Plato, Aristotle had a well-formed and remarkably modern sense of audiences: an essential asset in the analysis of identification. A recurring theme in *Rhetoric* is that audiences need to be intensively studied. Where Plato was notoriously suspicious of the arts for their imitative and emotional qualities,[12] Aristotle was far more accepting of the invitation art offers to audiences to step into the world of the "possible" or "probable."[13]

If we follow the lead of Burke in assessing *Rhetoric,* Aristotle emerges as a master psychologist of identification. The business of identification is nothing less than the central generative process in the design of messages. Burke's view arguably understates Aristotle's emphasis on rhetoric as a form of rational argumentation, and overstates his interest in adaptive appeals. Indeed, there is little in *Rhetoric* that could be directly translated into synonyms for "identification." But there can be no quarrel with the larger assumption imbedded in *Rhetoric, Topics, Poetics,* and *Prior Analytics* that rhetorical appeals must be conceived in terms of how they are received by their audiences. Persuasion, notes Aristotle, "must take into account the nature of . . . [a] particular audience."[14] Audiences are the "judges" of messages.[15] *Their* understanding of the good, the virtuous, and the true are the fundamental starting points for a successful rhetor.

Aristotle offers three broad strategies of appeal that are especially relevant to the process of rhetorical courtship. They are worthy of a brief review for their own insights, and because Burke attaches so much importance to their implicit embrace of the processes of identification.

The first involves the persuader's search for signs of character *(ethos)* that are compelling and attractive. For Aristotle "character may almost be called the most effective means of persuasion" an advocate possesses.[16] Although he criticized others for having neglected the role of the advocate, a concern for displaying the manifest signs of virtuous character is a constant that runs through most ancient rhetorics. In ways large and small a persuader must present himself and those he would praise as having virtues an audience would share. "If an audience esteems a given quality, we must say that our hero has that quality, no matter whether we are addressing Scythians or Spartans or philosophers."[17] There is simply no way to dismiss the powerful impulse of audiences to interpret messages through the filter of a source's *ethos.* Narrative and many other forms of public discourse continually draw us in by offering the details of private lives that identification makes us care about. We see it in Annie Dillard's affectionate memoir about her childhood in a leafy and comfortable Pittsburgh neighborhood. Her world is anchored by the details of her parents lives.[18] Over the course of her book we come to admire the habits and customs of a couple that managed to shun the conventionality of the Eisenhower years while successfully launching their children into adulthood.

A second implied form of identification comes from the use of *topoi* and "commonplaces," which were described by Aristotle as "notions possessed by everybody," hence self-evident. Sayings, maxims, and ideas widely adopted by a society were presented as the elemental materials of persuasion: a kind of ethnography of accepted attitudes.[19] And so we get a virtual catalogue of beliefs common to the audiences of his day, ranging from the young to the old.

At the extremes, for example, older men "guide their lives too much by considerations of what is useful and too little by what is noble." They "live by memory rather than by hope." And "they are continually talking of the past, because they enjoy remembering it."[20] For youth these ways of thinking tend to be reversed, but are just as clearly defined. In either case the rhetor's task is to duplicate the audience's attitude or preference in their own words.

To be sure, time often dates the common wisdom of another age. Yet the principle of locating beliefs shared by an audience is central to the process of identification. A primary feature of cultural studies ranging from ethnology to marketing research is the systematic cataloging of social beliefs and customs. They proceed from the solid assumption that what a society takes to be true or preferable functions as a crucial medium of exchange in public life.[21]

The third strategy is the construction of ideas using a reasoning sequence that begins from what is widely accepted and moves to new conclusions the advocate wants an audience to reach. Aristotle described this pathway of reasoning as an "enthymeme." Enthymemes function as the everyday equivalents of a logical syllogism. But where syllogisms are often admired for their rigor and the force of their conclusions, enthymemes exist in the more contingent nature of real-world settings. In their most basic form, they use reasoning patterns that start from a reservoir of common knowledge represented by signs or more group-specific commonplaces. These statements engage an audience by using beliefs or the imperfect knowledge they already have. Hence, "an enthymeme is a syllogism starting from probabilities or signs," such that one could argue "that a woman is with child because she is pale."[22] Like most enthymemes, the sign is inadequate and the conclusion is obviously far from certain.[23] But it is important to note that Aristotle was clearly captivated by what might be described as the logic of identification: reasoning that uses norms and accepted customs to win over adherents. Anyone who has assessed how we initiate a conversation with a stranger senses the many versions of this form as it exists in everyday life. We may break an awkward silence with a comment on the weather. A communication structure that moves from the recognizable to the new is a mechanism of daily survival. We reach for the familiar first: a subject that allows us to place the stranger in the context we already share.

An enthymeme that includes "common knowledge" tames our fear of difference and separation. It uses a reasoning sequence that starts from what is already "known" before moving to ideas or conclusions that might be contentious. The commonplace is a "foot in the door," the first step in a sequence of statements that ask for agreement and (often) acceptance of the source.

An additional feature of enthymemes speaks to Aristotle's sensitivity to the way actual appeals often work. He notes that acceptance of a statement is sometimes so assured that "there is no need to mention it. The hearer adds it himself."[24] The context of the topic is enough to trigger one's memory of the recent past or a relevant commonplace. For example, the spoken dialogue of a David Mamet screenplay often captures the shared experiences communicated in simple stares and unfinished sentences. In films like *Heist, A Life in the Theater,* and *Glengarry Glen Ross* characters talk in fragments. And yet we understand that they are bound to the same world of understandings. Similarly, an advocate for stricter gun laws may start a persuasive attempt with a chain of statements that begin with the observation that too many children die each year from gunshot wounds; or a prochoice speaker might state that too many children are born to couples who lack the means to be effective parents. In each case the first statement starts from common knowledge or widely accepted beliefs, and only then moves to related but more controversial conclusions.

In their totality these three components of revealed character, shared attitudes, and reasoning from common assumptions exist as core elements in the central canon of rhetoric. "As ideas," notes Burke, "they all seem no less compelling now than they ever were."[25] But it is important to note that identification is more than calculated similarity. Burke understood the mechanics of recognition and empathy used by Aristotle and other ancient rhetoricians to be only part of a larger process he labeled consubstantiality. In important ways that we will revisit again in the next chapter, identification is not simply a condition where *A* is identical with *B,* but where individuals come to believe they share "common sensations, concepts, images, ideas, attitudes."[26] Identification thus moves beyond the "externals" of similarity to deeper levels of unity. We are, at various times, "joined and separate, at once a distinct substance and consubstantial with another."[27] Thus, a grandchild may identify with a grandparent, a man with a woman, a Muslim with a Jew, and so on. All presume the capacity to assume the place of others who are outwardly very different from ourselves.

The surprising emergence of singer Johnny Cash as a lesbian icon carries the same feature of being more about "resonance" than similarity. He connects to this audience, notes one writer, through songs that chronicle "masculinity gone strange with grief, remorse, and loneliness."[28] It is an unlikely pairing of source and audience, but less so if we give full credit to the restless human capacity to find resonance in unlikely places. At a very different level the tendency of Japanese workers to identify with their employers speaks to the same process. Although a weakened economy has sometimes strained old loyalties, employers and workers often act on the assumption of consubstantiality. As Edwin Reischauer has noted, "A job in Japan is not merely a contractual arrangement for pay, but a means of identification with a larger entity—in other words, a satisfying sense of being part of something big and significant."[29]

Roots in the Pre-Socratic Sophists

One can go even further back in time to find earlier recognition of the centrality of identification to the persuasive process. Aristotle's teacher, Plato, reviled his own competitors and predecessors partly for their alleged indifference to truth in the process of winning over audiences. Plato's *Gorgias* takes as its central character a Sophist born about 490 B.C. who wrote manuals of rhetorical instruction and performed speeches to admiring audiences of his day. What we know about Gorgias is from incomplete fragments of his own work, and partly from the hostile dialogues of Plato.

For the great philosopher, Gorgias was a figure who lacked sufficient appreciation for the difficulties of teaching *arete'*, or the "qualities of human excellence" that produce natural leaders. *The Gorgias* wants us to worry about sophistic liberalism that gives legitimacy to the variability of public attitudes and to a persuader's efforts to deal with them. In Plato's view, catering to audience attitudes is not a virtue but a vice. He writes the heroic part of the dialogue for Socrates, who describes rhetoric as "a knack" for "ornamentation and sophistry," an art with more regard for "flattery" than truth. "Flattery" is represented as virtually coextensive with rhetoric: a form of pandering that gives pleasure to an audience and power to the persuader, but shuns allegiance to a higher morality.[30]

At a simplistic level it is hard to quarrel with Plato. Who could deny that identification has its uses as a tool of deception? With regard to the public discourse of politics and advertising, we pride ourselves on our cynicism. We know the wolf is in sheep's clothing, and that there are deeper and contradictory motivations behind the universal appeals we want to expose. Virtually all human action—and especially human expression—is subject to doubts about the potential gaps between stated and deeper intentions. So every act has its manifest meaning and alternative narratives. One can even deconstruct Plato's dialogue with its own ironic backstory. His unflattering portraits of his own contemporaries gives them words they may have never said, and at the same time, returns power and prestige to himself.

W. K. C. Guthrie's convincing analysis of the Sophist's career is more generous. He notes that Gorgias was among the first to place communication at the center of institutions that are primarily about verbal action, and at the same time recognizing the principle of adaptation as the bond that links an audience to an advocate.

> [Gorgias] saw the power of persuasion as paramount in every field, in the study of nature and philosophical subjects no less than in the law-courts or the political arena. One essential to the art was the sense of occasion, *kairos*, the right time or opportunity.[31]

Guthrie notes that there was a remarkably modern conception of culture behind some of the thinking of many of the Sophists, including Gorgias, Isocrates, Critias, Protagoras and others. It involves drawing a distinction between opposing worldviews in the organization of knowledge: two very different ways of thinking about the place of humans in the evolution of ideas. A view accepted by many of the Sophists held that "laws, customs and conventions were not part of the immutable order of things," but the products of the culture and its attitudes.[32] This realm of socially created law (*nomos*) was in sharp contrast to philosophies and assumptions that presented certain moral codes and truths of the natural world (*physis*) as *prior* to human understanding and awareness. The first gives priority to socially derived values and knowledge. The sec-

ond suggests larger forces—the Gods and natural law—as the ultimate arbiters of truth and value. Was religion a matter of social
convention, or did the gods really exist? Did states evolve through
the variable efforts and ideas of political organizations, or were
they conceived according to some divine plan? And is the division between slaves and masters solely the product of the values
and economies of particular culture, or the result of some higher
natural law?[33]

The Platonic quest for immutable truths often assumed the
existence of "unwritten laws" of moral conduct that were to be
discovered more than constructed. These starting points made it
easy for Plato to retain suspicions about democratic institutions.
There was simply no reason to consider collective public opinion
as reliably useful.[34] In modern life the fundamentalist's observation
that homosexuality is "unnatural" and not part of "God's plan"
draws from the same assumptions of unwritten law. Humans are
not the agents of their own societies. Larger forces and larger immutable values are at work.

But for Sophists who upheld the centrality of *nomos*, civil life
and social norms were seen as governed by the flow of human
events. Laws are the work of humans, not the gods. Moral precepts
are a matter of public opinion and custom rather than absolutes.
"Man is the measure of all things," declared Protagoras. The statement is a fitting epigram for the modernist assumption that civil life
is socially constructed. Burke's seminal "definition of man" (see
chapter 2) is a similar declaration of the dominance of the symbolic
world in our lives. It gives the same priority to culture as a construction of "symbol using (and mis-using) animals" who are thus
separated from their natural condition by instruments of their own
making.[35] Both views implicitly emphasize the importance of discourse as generative of culture. And both give greater weight to
identification as a process that binds a collectivity to the same
common experiences. We are civilized into the same culture, secur-
ing our place within it by finding ways to negotiate our differences
and demonstrate our similarities.

Much more could be said about the centrality of identification
in the history of rhetoric.[36] Even so, this sketch is at least suggestive
of its roots in early figures who understood our psychological impulse for consensus. In a nonrhetorical world individuals would

measure themselves against standards derived from outside the context of social conventions. But in a rhetorical world we are heavily invested in the values and language of our communities. We rarely escape their influence, though we are often active agents in interpreting their meaning.

Identification, Role-Taking and the Search for Self

Folding identification into the larger notion of adaptation takes us beyond any single intellectual thread. If the Hellenic world three hundred years before Christ generated an understanding of audiences as the owners of opinions which must be addressed, we will find no similar timelines that allow us to track the awareness of collective or individual identities. One thread leads us into the biochemical processes of pattern recognition in humans and related species: a topic best left to neuroscience. Another begs for a general scheme that accounts for how identity is shaped, and how it is maintained through consciousness of culture and community.

George Herbert Mead has noted that consciousness of the self is possible only with a concurrent consciousness of others. We are not simply "ourselves," but constructions shaped through our inter-actions with others. We use the materials of our relations with others to round out our sense of who we are. In Mead's words, "This requires the appearance of the other in the self, the identification of the other with the self, the reaching of self-consciousness through the other."[37] Language induces an awareness of "I," "we," and "they," even while it reflects features of the community back into the self.

This perspective represents a common theme running through much of our understanding of the nature of identity. *Who* we are to ourselves and to others is a collection of attributes assembled and discarded over a lifetime, a mosaic of impressions given off to others and held inside. At times we may appear to others pretty much as we see ourselves. John Kennedy once described Daniel Webster as the embodiment of a great man: "He looked like one, talked like one, was treated like one and insisted that he was one."[38] As we might say about someone today, he seemed to be "comfortable in his skin." But it is more likely that our internal and external "selves" are never fully integrated or consistent. They are always under reconstruction in ways that seek to negotiate the differences between who we are and who we want to be. When film star Cary Grant was reminded by fans that he personified the kind of person that many of them wanted to be, he noted wryly that "Everybody wants to be Cary Grant . . . *I* want to be Cary Grant."[39] His point, of course, was that his sophisticated on-screen character was the artful abstraction of a much more complex Archie Leach, who would go through four painful divorces and never live so perfect an off-screen life.

Mead notes what has since become a basic paradigm of communication: that a communicator and audience are involved in one large and imperfect feedback loop. The communicator "is influenced by the attitudes of those about him, which are reflected back into the different members of the audience so that they come to respond as a whole."[40] In this process "He himself is in the role of the other person whom he is . . . influencing."[41] In short, the public self is a unique construction that has been negotiated between the private self and what we believe audiences expect of us.

This role-taking model is not without its problems, particularly when placed in a psychological framework. Several concerns are relevant. Some social theorists have questioned the value of placing communication at the center of the construction of the self.[42] Language may be a reflection of who we are, but is not necessarily synonymous with it. There is a certain elasticity of labeling and identity such that a person may accept a characterization of themselves, say, as "gifted" or "hard working," even if they doubt the accuracy of the description. Others, like Anselm Strauss, also note that we need a more subtle way to talk about identities, particularly the interactions between "personal histories" and "social histories." A person "must be viewed as embedded in a temporal matrix not simply of his own making, but . . . his conception of the past as it impinges on himself."[43]

Strauss's concerns are especially relevant to the legacy of Sigmund Freud, who—as Burke notes—almost inadvertently enriched the language for the rhetorical analysis of identification while looking at meaning derived from personal experience. Even though his theories of emotional development have been discredited by many, Freud's conception of identification as "an emotional tie with another person" remains central to any understanding of the term.[44] And his *Interpretation of Dreams* was important in establishing a rationale for seriously considering the verbal and symbolic baggage of everyday life, including popular stories, legends, and evocative symbols.[45] One does not have to accept all aspects of the Freudian canon to appreciate his explorations of how consciousness is modulated by a subject's life history. But his primary emphasis on developmental processes associated with identity formation is too reductive and deterministic to fully account for the construction of meaning and significance in the temporal environments of public discourse and popular culture. This newer "cultural meanings" context is not irrelevant to older Freudian ideas of identity formation. But—at least for this writer—one does not easily telescope into the other.

With its core themes of the reciprocity of ideas and attitudes, the importance of the role-taking model is undeniable. We are audiences to each other, constructing and defining ourselves to meet the expectations of others. In various ways role taking is fundamental to understanding the daily give and take of social relations.[46] It clearly represents an irreplaceable metaphor for the rhetorical process of identification. To a substantial extent we are nurtured, maintained, and sometimes undermined by the sum of our interactions with others. Our individual biographies can be read as maps that allow us to retrace our influences. We acquire our values from culture and opinions from our immediate contacts. And we learn from our responses to life's exigencies. To be sure, these acquisitions of insights based on real-world experiences are never reflexive. To define someone as the "product" of Catholic schools, the Upper West Side of Manhattan, or a small town in eastern Wyoming is not enough to claim an understanding of them. And no one would want to be known simply by these identifiers. But even these incomplete facts have their own power to establish and sometimes undermine expectations.

It would be difficult to overestimate the potency of expectations as they are affirmed and violated. Expectations affirmed are often identifications. Expectations denied are potentially sources of alienation. Consider, for example, the case of the iconic John Wayne. A roadhouse a few miles from my home has framed pictures of the actor bedecked in cowboy garb hanging on the walls at each end of the bar. One assumes that Wayne has pride of place in this largely male refuge because of what he represents to the owner and his patrons. Wayne grew up in California and came to symbolize the West as both a place and a state of mind. In the settled East a person had to adapt to existing laws and customs. But a Westerner once had to be more resourceful and independent to survive in a region where the land and its inhabitants had not yet been tamed. Or so went the myth. And so we have romanticized Wayne's film persona through these familiar impressions and attitudes. The hero of *Stagecoach* and *The Alamo* used and enhanced fantasies Americans still cling to about the men and women who would not easily submit to the harsh western landscape. The figure of Wayne on horseback moving through an unbroken sea of sagebrush and rimrocks easily fits into this world.

But, as Garry Wills notes, Wayne was also another person who was significantly at odds with this image. That he was born in Iowa with the less mellifluous name of Marion Morrison—and actually hated horses—is a reminder of how some identifications are nourished and others are not.[47] He also went out of his way to avoid interrupting his Hollywood career for military service during World War II, a somewhat surprising fact given his love of the military roles. But such is the nature of all role-taking. It selectively constructs a presence that can feed our interest in prospecting for its paradoxical opposites. Old film stars are especially fertile ground for these explorations. In Burke's phrase, a rhetoric of identification also implicitly invites us "to confront the implications of division."[48]

Identification and the Dramatic Imperative

In his classic study, *The Presentation of Self in Everyday Life*, Erving Goffman used overt dramatic terminology to extend the idea of roles acquired through audience-mediated communication. In the presence of others, he notes, we typically "project" a "definition of the situation" as we see it. That definition usually carries a number of expectations we believe others hold about what the totality of our behavior (language, gesture, appearance, and attitude) should be. In Goffman's dramatistic scheme, situations carry a performance imperative: we know how we should act. We have a sense of how to manage our identity, our "front," and how others are supposed to perceive it. We play off of that identity to "manage" the "impressions" we give to others. In short, we are performers in search of receptive audiences. "Thus, when the individual presents himself before others, his performance will tend to incorporate and exemplify the officially accredited values of the society, more so, in fact than does his behavior as a whole."[49]

Implicit is the image of the self as a collection of multiple roles. These features of our identity are on display as each occasion demands it. We fashion elements of our performance to meet the exigencies of social life as they occur. One enters a new social setting with a natural interest to succeed in it. In colloquial terms, "screwing up," "laying an egg," "making a scene," or "pulling it off," are suggestive of a range of possible outcomes. In life as in the theater, the actor's first responsibility is to seem to inhabit fully the role he or she is performing. We do not want to see someone struggling to meet the expectations of their role. We are more comfortable if we feel that they have completely taken ownership of it. This was ostensibly President Reagan's special gift. He certainly knew the script of the presidency, and his relaxed affability suggested that he was at home there. But over time these images of confidence could be undermined as it was when observers noticed Reagan's periodic glances to staff-written answers to questions concealed in a partly opened desk drawer.[50] Was the President the product of his "handlers," as the national press largely assumed? Or was his appeal in his apparent authenticity?

The significance of the role as a model for examining the possibilities of identification is suggested in Hugh Duncan's observation, building on Mead, that drama is the "means by which we become objects to ourselves."[51] This statement is a wonderful evocation of the power for identification inherent in drama. The attraction of theater, film, or the novel lies partly in their abilities to give audiences potent commentaries on their own values and choices. In Duncan's words, "The novel presents a situation which lies outside the immediate experience of the reader in a form which makes it possible for him to enter into the attitudes of the groups in the situation."[52]

For example, as I note in more detail in chapter 3, dramatists talk of the "emotional center" of a work to suggest that point at which an audience is meant to become "one" with a character and the situation he or she inhabits. Narratives usually include a character that acts as a vessel for transporting us into a different world. Jonathan Harr's novelistic account of an actual case of litigation against polluters in *A Civil Action* provides such a port of entry.[53] Years of legal maneuvering over the suspicious deaths of children in Woburn, Massachusetts are distilled in the book. Lawyers are reluctant to accept the case of the families, until it is discovered that the polluters are owned by two corporations with deep pockets for a potential settlement.

That is the basic story, but its emotional center resides in characters like the stubborn Boston lawyer who took the case on a contingency fee basis, only to end up in bankruptcy after covering his investigation expenses. Readers are meant to identify with him and the victims of the pollution. The corporations are the unsympathetic enemies in a continuing high-stakes chess game. Harr's novel holds a mirror to the idea of financial compensation for victims, finding that objective a hopelessly inadequate basis for delivering true justice. But we are essentially coaxed into considering the problem because of the drama of the characters who, not unlike ourselves, must make choices with significant consequences. The appeal of the narrative comes from its characters, rather than the political and legal processes to which they are tied.

Narratives of national life also make us objects to ourselves. Impressions of national events usually come to us through the polarizing or unifying presence of specific agents. The 2001 attacks on the World Trade Center and Pentagon created a thin but obvious sense of national unity. The human loss at a fourteen-acre site in lower Manhattan was enough by itself to conclude that the nation as a whole had been attacked. Deep national differences were largely set aside in favor of expressions of communal unity and grief. By contrast, in the corrosive national environment of 1998, very different forces were at work. Americans confronted portrayals of the actions of President Bill Clinton, Independent Prosecutor Kenneth Starr, and other players in concurrent sex and impeachment dramas. Denials of various improprieties by the president where met by aggressive and sometimes small-minded investigation techniques that sharpened differences in Congress and the nation. Did this national nightmare feed a growing sense of alienation from our national life? How do these events fit into what we want to believe about our collective past? As Robert Bellah and his colleagues note,

"If we face a crisis of civic identity, it is not just a social crisis, it is a personal crisis as well."[54] The death and national trauma of September 11 momentarily reversed the nation's withered sense itself. But the whole extended impeachment episode weakened rather than enhanced American confidence in its civic institutions.

The inevitable cycles of civic engagement and disengagement have been productively explored by others, and is the subject of chapter 6.[55] Their relevance here lies in the fact that issues like these are—in their simplest form—at the center of what the rest if this book is about: a sense of connectedness or the lack of it; of fragmented pieces of identity affirmed or denied.

The task that remains, then, is to flesh out the idea of identification as a pivot point in communication, taking on the same mission of discovery that energized Kenneth Burke. Burke quoted the words of St. Augustine, who noted that a person is persuaded if

> he likes what you promise, fears what you say is imminent, hates what you censure, embraces what you commend, regrets whatever you built up as regrettable, rejoices at what you say is cause for rejoicing, sympathizes with those whose wretchedness your words bring before his very eyes . . . and in whatever ways your high eloquence can affect the minds of your hearers.[56]

Augustine's premise of building common ground illustrates the central theme of this chapter as well. At its core, identification is a moment of recognition that links a person to someone else. It usually represents a heightened awareness of the relevance of one's own life to a parallel setting inhabited by others: a natural outgrowth of our tendency to find our way in life by reflecting the actions of others back on to ourselves. In its highest form identification offers the potent sensation of sharing another's consciousness. In the process, it diminishes the distance between the alien and the known, providing a sense of "place" for ourselves in the external world.

Freud, Mead, and Burke extended identification into new ways of thinking about the construction and reconstruction of the self. The goal of this study is to build on their work, while placing identification in more contemporary contexts. The deeper structures of identification are the central concerns of the next two chapters. The last three apply elements of these structures to cases from the worlds of politics, art, and social action.

Chapter 2

CONCEPTUALIZING
IDENTIFICATION

Extensions of a Burkean View

Rhetoric . . . is rooted in an essential function of language itself, a function that is wholly realistic, and continually born anew; the use of language as a symbolic means of inducing cooperation in beings that by nature respond to symbols.
—Kenneth Burke, *A Rhetoric of Motives*

The subtlety of his critical work has challenged, its perversity has provoked, its original insights have opened up immense corridors of thought. Nobody who is capable of following him at all plodges in his footsteps; he is a critic for the adventurous, you take from him what you can get, and only realize later how much that was.
—Robert Adams describing Kenneth Burke

From a communications perspective, arguably the most important theorist of identification was Kenneth Burke, whose influence on rhetorical and cultural criticism has been enormous. Burke's lifelong speculations on the mediating nature of language was influenced by the intellectual firmament of his time. Writing his most important work between the 1930s and early 1950s, he absorbed the canon of modernist thought in the work of Freud, Mead, Marx, Veblen, and others, at the same time using critiques of socially generated meaning to create an extended view of the province of rhetoric.[1] Rhetoric should not be known primarily for its ability to obscure the truth (though, to be sure, he understood such uses), but for how its "resources of ambiguity" could "induce cooperation" or "transcend differences." For Burke communication lies at the very core of our sociality. We cannot escape—and, indeed, should embrace—the rhetorical construction of consciousness.

Burke was not alone in viewing the centrality of language to the matrix of a culture.[2] But few did it with a greater sense of intellectual freedom and playful adventure. He has justifiably been credited for playing a pivotal role in the discovery of the "hidden history" of rhetoric, triggering its reestablishment as an important area of study.[3] His somewhat surprising adoption by rhetoricians in many large but moribund English and speech departments helped regenerate these fields, aided by early interpreters such as Hugh Dalziel Duncan, Bernard Brock, Marie Hochmuth Nichols, and William Rueckert.

In what he described as his own intellectual "wanderings," he offered a rich range of possibilities to consider in describing the rhetoric of association and estrangement. In its totality, the Burkean scheme amounted to an explicit repudiation of the rising tide of academic behaviorism of his day, and an invitation to communication and social theorists to find an ontological basis for rhetoric. In the spirit of his work, this chapter is both a recapitulation of some of those ideas, and an attempt to probe their possibilities and inadequacies. The larger first part of the chapter explores his theories of identification and association. The second part moves somewhat beyond Burke's emphasis on the resources of language to a consideration of identification's effects and limits.

Language as "Equipment for Living"

Burke was not a linear thinker, nor an analyst who could be defined by a single methodology. He often approached subjects from oblique angles, as in his description of Marxist thought not as a sociohistorical account of class and culture, but "a critique of capitalist rhetoric."[4] The complex fabric of his work resists categorization in the lexicography of any one field. He was—in the best and broadest sense of the word—an undisciplined theorist. Much of his work shows the influence of other fields with similar assumptions about the a priori nature of language, including general semantics, the sociology of knowledge, and linquistics. Never one to honor tight disciplinary boundaries, Burke nonetheless wove many of their ideas into his work, combining an anthropologist's interest in magic, religion, and class with a literary critic's skill for the "close reading" of texts. Readers of his eclectic work find themselves in the presence of a thinker in the tradition of the Sophists: a scholar who placed symbolic action at the presumptive center rather than the periphery of human events.[5]

In his view, language creates and sustains its own reality. Our "natural vocation" is the construction and maintenance of an identity where words are not simply the names for things, but "entitlements" conferred or denied. Language is not derivative of human experience, but is—in many ways—prior to it.[6] His pivotal "definition of man" uses telegraphic language to communicate his starting points. In typical Burkean fashion, he provides a closely reasoned account of this definition, as well as an epigram to summarize it:[7]

> Being bodies that learn language
> Thereby becoming wordlings
> Humans are the
> Symbol-making, symbol-using, symbol-misusing animal
> Inventor of the negative
> Separated from our natural
> Condition by instruments of our own making
> Goaded by the spirit of hierarchy
> Acquiring foreknowledge of death
> And rotten with perfection[8]

The definition captures what Burke finds unique about our species: its "logological" obsession, and the consequent placement of the symbolic over the physical as the dominant measure of our identity. Our capacity for symbolic action in language sets humans apart from the rest of the world. The "reductive, abstractive, metaphorical, analytic, and synthesizing powers of all language" invites us to occupy another plane of existence.[9] Language not only allows us to recreate the events and sensations of the physical world, but its infinitely suggestive rhetorical nature pushes us to use its resources to impose our wishes on it. As an instrument for praise and blame, it makes perfection internally knowable if not externally achievable. It provides a rich palate of negatives and "shalt nots" to portray what is missing or "immoral" in our world. It thus "separates us from our natural condition by instruments of our making," providing the "equipment" for a consciousness that allows us to narrate our history, comment on our failings, and see our own mortality. The rhetorical alteration of this consciousness in large and small ways is the primary business of identification.

A Conceptual Baseline: Identification as Strategic Adaptation

Burke's preoccupation with identification began with an interest in audiences, and the ways they relate to *form* and structure. As Sheron Pattison notes, his move from literary criticism to rhetorical analysis was abetted by his interest in making the audience a necessity rather than an adjunct of literary expression.[10] Looking back over his own career, Burke recalled that "things started moving for me in earnest when, as attested in *Counter-Statement*, I made the shift from 'self expression' to 'communication.' "[11] Art grounded in aesthetics apparently became less interesting than art as a vehicle for shaping audience attitudes and emotions. An interest in form was the pivot point. Among a variety of meanings he assigns to form is the central idea that it encompasses a familiar landscape of "universals" and "conditions of appeal."[12] A work has form, he notes, "insofar as one part of it leads a reader to anticipate another part, to be gratified by the sequence."[13] The resulting "collaborative expectancy" between source and audience can become a kind of bond.

> For instance, imagine a passage built about a set of oppositions ("*we* do this, but *they* on the other hand do *that*; *we* stay *here*, but *they* go *there*; *we* look *up*, but *they* look *down*," etc.). Once you grasp the trend of the form, it invites participation regardless of the subject matter. Formally, you will find yourself swinging along with the succession of antitheses, even though you may not agree with the proposition that is being presented in this form.[14]

Burke's focus on strategies of appeal eventually became the primary idea behind his goal to reinvigorate rhetoric theory by shifting its old emphasis on "persuasion" to the more encompassing idea of "identification." A reference to the words of W. C. Blum suggests the additional "openings" he envisioned by his choice of the newer word, with its broader political and sociopsychological associations: "In identification lies the source of dedications and enslavements, in fact all cooperation."[15]

Over the course of his lifetime, Burke repeatedly amended his explanations of the ways rhetoric can induce agreement. But he started with the more simple and essential Aristotelian notion that rhetoric requires the search for common ground with an audience. Quoting Aristotle's aphorism that "it is not hard to praise Athenians among Athenians," Burke notes that the search for shared elements of good character and common themes (*topoi* and commonplaces) offer the "simplest case of persuasion."

> You persuade a man only insofar as you can talk his language in speech, gesture, tonality, order, image, attitude, idea, *identifying* your ways with his. Persuasion by flattery is but a special case of persuasion in general.[16]

This theme also appears in the ancient rhetorics and philosophies of Aristotle, Cicero, Quintilian, and others.[17]

Other moderns looking at the strategic uses of communication also understand the centrality of appeals to similarity. Writing in 1917, James Winans notes, "To convince or persuade a man is largely a matter of identifying the opinion or course of action which you wish him to adopt with one or more of his fixed opinions or customary courses of action. When his mind is satisfied of the identity, then doubts vanish."[18] Robert Oliver's classic 1942 text, *The Psychology of Persuasive Speech* similarily spends time discussing the nature of "common ground," with the objective of exploring "the possibilities of avoiding arguments" that might get in the way of a speaker's success.[19] Seekers of compromise or consensus might find at least four pathways to explore, including common interests, shared feelings, shared beliefs, and similar methods.[20] All focus on extrinsic means or tactics for establishing an affinity between audiences and their supplicants. And all suggest that identification is a problem of message design, a matter of clothing one's own views in a way that establishes their acceptability for others.

Burke incorporated similar ideas in his own work, and they are part of the definition I offered earlier in chapter 1. This adaptive impulse is what might be called the central imperative of rhetoric *as addressed* to others. But, as most of Burke's interpreters have discovered, he was loath to be pinned down by any single definition.

Bernard Brock notes that Burke's evolution "from the criticism of literature, to a criticism of rhetoric, and finally to a criticism of philosophy" is reflected in the increasingly broad epistemological claims made for rhetoric.[21] A similar elasticity is evident from his later summary of three meanings for identification, which range from the strategic effects implied in my definition, to "unnoticed" effects and that fall beyond its proviso of "conscious awareness":

> The first is quite dull. It flowers in such usages as that of a politician who, though rich, tells humble constituents of his humble origins. The second kind of identification involves the workings of antithesis, as when allies who would otherwise dispute among themselves join forces against a common enemy. This application also can serve to deflect criticism, a politician can call any criticism of his policies "unpatriotic," on the grounds that it reinforces the claims of the nation's enemies. But the major power of "identification" derives from situations in which it goes unnoticed. My prime example is the word "we," as when the statement that "we" are at war includes under the same head soldiers who are getting killed and spectators who hope to making a killing in war stocks.[22]

Reduced to their simplest terms, these three forms might be labeled as "similarity," "commonality," and "terms that hide division." Add "identification through grammatical and generic forms," which we discussed earlier, and one can see four distinct types.

All are clearly useful. But Burke's bold assertion that "the major power of identification derives from situations that go *unnoticed*" poses a problem. To be sure, he picks a compelling example of language used to cover over division with a thin veneer of unity. But with this case I believe Burke telescopes the meaning of identification to the outer limits of its natural range. His value as a critic is seen in his sensitivity for the ways deterministic language passes unnoticed through rhetors and audiences.[23] Fair enough. Language has a host of fascinating social functions that are not managed by individual agents, and—building on the work of Freud, Marx, and others—Burke was superbly adept at seeing them. Indeed, explorations of how thought is silently infused with the language of gender, class, and hierarchy represents a dominant critical paradigm for assessing all forms of cultural products. But from the standpoint of rhetoric and poetics as art, I find it difficult to extend identifications into realms not consciously processed by rhetors or receivers. Motives and meanings may be latent, but in the words of my earlier definition in chapter 1, identifications typically work by asking for heightened awareness or by revisiting a feeling or state of mind we already know. They seek to engage the consciousness of the auditor, and they count phenomenologically as a kind of experience. Rhetoric as a method of sociolinquistic analysis plays a vital role in finding latent meanings and smuggled assumptions. But rhetoric as an art assumes the presence of engaged and coactive audiences. To be affected by the supercharged meanings of identification, audiences must be more than somnolent targets. To make identifications wholly or partially subliminal renders the traditional stipulation that rhetoric must act on audiences who are free to make their own choices almost meaningless.[24]

Burke's Sociology of Verbal Transcendence

Subsumed in the idea of identification is the "complementary" process of separation. As William Rueckert notes, division and unification are two sides of the same coin. "Existence is a kind of dialectic of division and merger, disintegration and reintegration, death and rebirth, war and peace . . ."[25] Various rhetorics may encompass differences that sharpen or bridge distinctions in the realms of religion, politics, and class. On the downside, they can exist "in the region of the scramble of insult and injury, bickering, squabbling, malice, and the lie, cloaked malice and the subsidized lie."[26] On the upside, our discourse naturally feeds on a "logological entelechy" that makes perfection possible in language if not in life. We aspire to the best or the better because our language makes it possible. A rhetoric of religion is therefore not simply words for and about God, but one of many possible frames of reference that can provide vocabularies of idealized states, of which "eternity" and "heaven" are only the most obvious examples.[27]

Conflicts can be bridged by rhetorical "acts of synthesis,"[28] which involve such artful constructions. Humans build "frames of acceptance or rejection by overt or covert acts of 'transcendence.' "[29] Burke's example of "we" as a substitute for "I" creates such a framework. The earlier term is corporate; it implies that the individual is part of a community. It also implies a sharing rather than a concentrating of power, suggesting a higher unity and perhaps concealing a contest for power. Identification thus grows out of the need to overcome conflict, difference, division, and competition. It serves as the primary mediating agent in the presence of divergent attitudes and motives. Without conflict, identification becomes a process without a purpose; with conflict, it becomes a necessity. As Burke notes,

> In pure identification there would be no strife. Likewise, there would be no strife in absolute separateness. . . . But put identification and division ambiguously together, so that you cannot know for certain just when one ends and the other begins, and you have the characteristic invitation to rhetoric.[30]

Consider the disputes that have continued to flare up since the end of the Vietnam War. The defeat of the American military was a defining moment for many who remain unsettled about American motives and the war's internal critics.[31] And the decisions of the Kennedy, Johnson, and Nixon administrations are widely discredited today. But opposition to the war has left many older Americans with divided loyalties: a fact reflected in an entire genre of Vietnam films, and in the strong emotions rekindled by the continuing celebrity of some former prisoners of war. One outcome of the Burkean approach is to search for levels of agreement that could transcend the dialectic of opposing factions. How can veterans who feel they never received the respect they deserved be reconciled with those who sought to avoid serving in an "immoral war"? At what point can differences be "put to rest" by appeals to shared values?

Bill Clinton's dramatic 1993 appearance before a Memorial Day audience on the sacred ground of the Vietnam Memorial in Washington provided one solution to the search for a transcendent appeal. This event is examined more closely in chapter 4, but it is interesting to note here that Clinton tried to make the required transcendent appeal. Soldiers have fought and died to protect our freedoms, he noted, including the freedom to dissent:

> Let us continue to disagree, if we must, about the war, but let us not let it divide us as a people any longer. No one has come here today to disagree about the heroism of those whom we honor, but the only way we can really honor their memory

is to resolve to live and serve today and tomorrow as best we can, and to make America the best that she can be.[32]

Like all such appeals, the hope was that the higher ground of shared commonplaces would reconnect divided factions.

For other divisive issues such as abortion, no similar transcending appeals are evident. Some issues seem to resist a point where factions will converge in values or beliefs that are inclusive for all. Laurence Tribe concludes his exhaustive study of the legal and rhetorical sides of the abortion debate by observing that this "clash of absolutes" yields only "a sliver of light in a world of shadow." In the end, he notes, neither side can fairly argue from a "presumption of correctness" for the "rights of the unborn fetus" or a "woman's right to choose."[33] The law and the rights that it guarantees is politically established and, as such, subject to legitimate amendment and change. And yet the most vocal in the debate assume this presumption of unchallengability, forestalling appeals that might bridge the space in between. Even so, identification is still a force if each side finds solidarity and community in its opposition to the other: what Burke described earlier as "identification through antithesis."[34]

Changing the Interpretive Frame: Ranges of Associations

The notion of transcendence is useful, but only gets us so far. It serves as a general indicator of the pathway to a language of cooperation, but it is a reductive shorthand for a process that has a range of rhetorical causes. Following a line of analysis suggested by Christine Oravec, it is possible to find additional subtleties of Burkean identification in three sub-groups loosely laid out in *The Rhetoric of Motives*.[35] In his discussions of the "rhetoric of class" he uses each one to represent increasingly abstract realms of association.

The simplest involves what he describes as *mechanical* linkages between a sign and its socially accepted meaning. We are "trained by the conditions of living" to react in a certain "mechanical" way to specific cues. These associations may be "accidental," but have over time acquired the accumulated weight of conventional meaning. Signs and their referents may have a familiarity that makes them second nature, accepted without critical awareness. They are like "conditioned reflexes" and, as such, may pass through receivers at low levels of awareness. Thus a text that fascinated Burke, Veblen's *Theory of the Leisure Class,* shows that "People seem to be bent on doing and acquiring certain things simply because these things happen to have become the signs of an admired status."[36] Or we can establish a set of expected words or actions appropriate to a given "scene" or "agent." What Burke described as the "ratio" of expectations that exist between agents and acts, or between scenes and acts, is proscribed by culture and custom.[37] Certain linkages have become familiar and mechanical. In our time a woman who identifies her profession as "health care" might be, reflexively if incorrectly, assumed to be a nurse. Fewer would make the same agent/act association for a man.

To call these routine associations true elements of the process of identification is technically correct, but mundane, since the static nature of predictable usage is less capable of producing the most interesting kinds of transformative moments. Since the very nature of the mechanistic response is its conventionality, it offers a greater chance for a lower-order "identification of" *something* than a higher-order "identification with" *someone.*[38]

A second level of *analogical* associations is "where terms are transferred from one order to another."[39] This form moves us into a more "imaginative" realm, where meaning is derived from moving a symbol from its common context to a more creative kind of reassignment. Analogical associations shift (or smuggle) terms of magic into science, religion into commerce or (as in Marxist ideology) politics into history. We have a nearly limitless ability to reassign meaning to a subject by reclothing it in the language and context of another.

Burke's examples are often focused on money and business, as when he notes that in "a business culture" the idea of "price" may be given equivalency to "value," the latter begging for acceptance as an aesthetic standard.[40]

> The same admonition should be introduced with regard to our reservations on technologism, as it is manifested in the cult of manufactured commodities (the doctrine that might be summed up: "It's culture if it's something you can buy")....Such symbols are not merely reflections of the

things symbolized, or signs for them; they are to a degree a *transcending* of the things symbolized.[41]

The novelty of the realignment of attitudes through language gets our attention, but it is our sense of their appropriateness that may strike strong chords of recognition. In Martin Luther King's most famous address he effectively used the analogy of a blank check to speak to the nation in language it understood. A moral imperative was redefined in terms in the inviolate language of commerce and contracts: a code of obligations King no doubt understood as basic to the American entrepreneurial soul. Speaking for the thousands of marchers spread out in front of him at the Lincoln Memorial, he noted that they had come to "cash a check" that supposedly guaranteed Negro rights:

> When the architects of our Republic wrote the magnificent words of the Constitution and the Declaration of Independence, they were signing a promissory note to which every American was to fall heir. This note was a promise that all men—yes, black men as well as white men—would be guaranteed the unalienable rights of life, liberty, and the pursuit of happiness.[42]

The infinite plasticity of language is, of course, the root of the appeal that "poetic" constructions have for us. The cumulative legacy of Burke's intellectual output is partly in the inventive ways he demonstrates our natural tendency to find new perspectives in the incongruities created by symbolic realignments.[43]

The third form of identification is described as *ideological*, where clusters of terms or symbols are "all derived from the same generating principle, hence all embodying it. . . ."[44] As Oravec notes, ideological identification occurs "when a single superstructural association serves as a basis for relating different concerns 'generically.' "[45] Money, to use Burke's central example, is itself much more than a medium of monetary exchange. It is rife with possibilities in terms of its "reductive, abstractive, and substitutive resources":

> Given an economic situation, there are ways of thinking that arise in response to it. But these ways of living and thinking, in complex relationship with both specific and generic motives, can go deep, to the level of principles. For

a way of living and thinking is reducible to terms of an "idea"—and that "idea" will be "creative" in the sense that anyone who grasps it will embody it or represent it in any mode of action he may choose.[46]

Veblen's portrayal of money as a motive for emulation provides a useful but imperfect system of thought for Burke. It suggests an explanation of material acquisition as a calculated source of envy (mechanistic association), while at the same time offering a cluster of attitudes in a more or less self-contained scheme for the interpretation of materialistic accumulation (ideological association). Virtually any systemic account of social and institutional behavior functions as an ideology, especially if it makes claims to completeness. Introduce but one word from an ideological nomenclature, and we might be stumped to identify it's sociohistorical home. But introduce two or three, and the context for their usage suddenly becomes much more evident. Thus the word "American" is ideologically ambiguous; the phrase "true American" is less so.

The potency of ideological associations like these can be seen in recent and raucous political debates about governmental funding of the arts. In the 1980s the art world and the federal endowment agencies were criticized in many quarters for allegedly having subverted themselves into realms foreign to their own best interests. Beginning with congressional complaints about homoerotic exhibits partly funded at public expense, conflict over the "ideological ownership" of art in America became especially intense.[47] Over subsequent years, feuds would flare up over issues ranging from whether to fund public television, to the wisdom of prosecuting museum directors for their roles in displaying "obscene" art. At the same time, institutions that ostensibly nurture and exhibit art became politicized, caught between congressional moralists who wanted its images to remain conventionally "safe," and social activists on the prowl for images that represent unjust victimization.

Each side pushed its own ideology, one out of the motive of representing the fragile sensibilities of "all" Americans ("family values," "basic decency"), the other out of the belief that particular groups within the larger culture (women, gays, African Americans) are too vulnerable to be portrayed in ways that risk their idealized identities ("political correctness," "multiculturalism").[48] The moralists gave us Senator Jesse Helms and his congressional allies who, among other things, tried to de-fund the National Endowment for the Arts (NEA) out of existence. The other side produced performance artists *cum* victims who believed "that mere expressiveness is enough," and that criticism of one's art is merely another form of victimage for one's identity.[49]

Robert Hughes sees each of these twin prongs as a vise that has made it difficult for professionals with legitimate standards (artists, museum curators, and critics) to function for the larger good of the artistic enterprise. But what he laments in the art world is what Burke describes as the natural tendency to impose on any field of activity an overlay of values and beliefs in service to a larger idea. The potency of the ideological forces at work in these "culture wars" armed both sides with a self-perpetuating system of evocative identifications. Each was partly held together by a shared sense of their own victimage at the hands of their opponents. In defiance of charges that they fostered "permissive" and "obscene" artists, progressives saw "censorship" from "religious nuts" "moral zealots," "fear brokers," and "right-wing homophobes."[50] At this level, Senator Helms was the perfect vessel to contain all of the attributions of backwater provincialism and know-nothing righteousness that congressional supporters of the arts associated with their opponents. Resistance to him was perhaps as affirming to those engaged in the battle to save the NEA as any of their own core ideas.

Identification as Identity Adjustment

Burke's discussion of the forms of identification and association provide a broad range of interesting and contrasting pathways to influence. In considering all three forms—mechanistic, analogical, and ideological—it becomes more apparent that the value of the latter two in particular lies in their potential power to induce change by reframing and renaming one's own experience. Analogical associations "reframe" by offering a shift in language that promotes a novel point of view on a familiar event or attitude. These kinds of associations might provoke the representative response, "I never thought about it that way before." Ideological associations "rename" by providing a coherent vocabulary of motives for actions that previously seemed incoherent. A typical response to such relabeling could take the form, "It's a different matter when you put it in those terms." Both are divergent routes to the same end, creating a new perspective that can alter a person's view of themselves in relation to their surroundings. And both share the potential of using language as a way to produce what I would call an *identity adjustment*. To say "my views have changed" is often to imply that there has been an identity shift as well: less cosmic, to be sure, than the evolution of the basic features of social or psychological identity, but significant nonetheless.

Identity is a mosaic of attributes and wishes we assign to ourselves. As Madan Sarup notes, it is "not something we find, or have once and for all." It more closely resembles "a kaleidoscope where the patterns are continuously changing."[51] If it is never fully knowable to the individual, its importance remains in the generative force of language to give it shape.

This adjustment of identity starts when a message puts an action or a personal situation in a different context, requiring a change in the relationship of the self to it. This new way of viewing or understanding the self then triggers a change in attitude.[52]

Consider the opposing rhetorics of motives that were implied by different interpretations of American conduct in Vietnam during the late 1960s. The war created a dialectic of opposites that reshaped attitudes, and then segments of identities. An increasingly fractured nation came to view the conflict either as a "battle against communist aggression," or as—as opponents often saw it—a "civil war" frozen in place by a dominating colonial power. To have abandoned the first characterization in favor of the second invited an identity shift as well. With a change of outlook there had to be concurrent changes in attitudes about the news reporting of the war, official assessments issued by the president and the military, and so on. Americans agonized over the role of the United States in Vietnam in part because commitment or opposition to the massive U.S. presence carried personal consequences. It was not uncommon for the issue to divide families and friends. And while outward manifestations of identity adjustment are not always easy to see, they were sometimes evident in small ways, such as in peasant garb favored at the time by the youthful New Left.

Drama, fiction, and especially film, play an important role in helping us understand the power and importance of identity transformations. Virtually all narratives are narratives of identity adjustment. As is noted in the next chapter, film and theater literally and figuratively make this process transparent. Characters coming to the end of Act III are rarely the same characters we observed in Act I. For the price of admission we are guaranteed a window that looks out on the lives of people in the risky business of remaking themselves. And because narrative presents a complete and more or less self-contained world, it provides its own ideology: its own universe of values and judgments. All combine to invite audiences to consider how the symbolic action of the plot *requires* the redefinition of a character's sense of self. What are the actions and accidents that will demand identity transformations? How did key agents in the story respond to the influences of others, and how did those events open or foreclose certain responses? Drama is full of such big and little epiphanies.

We find this process fascinating in its own terms, but also because it invites us to see in others what we recognize or imagine in ourselves. The behavior of melodrama's heroes and fools, victims and villains, is rarely a duplicate script of our own lives, but a kind of analogical extension of our own sensibilities into the world vividly recreated on the stage or screen. The transformation of a screen character mimics (and often idealizes) what the identification process would leave us to imagine if placed in the same circumstances: pragmatism transformed into heroism (*Casablanca*, *The Times of Harvey Milk*), detachment transformed into commitment (*Rear Window*, *In the Bedroom*), ideologies of dominance changed into an ideologies of equality (*Dances with Wolves*, *To Kill a Mockingbird*), and so on.

What film displays in technicolor also transpires in smaller and subtler ways in other aspects of our lives. For example, if I am induced to change my position on a political candidate, I am also obliged to carry the new identity of a supporter, especially if I make my voting intentions known to others.[53] My reasons for changing my mind may need to be reconciled with inconsistent parts of my older beliefs.[54] There is no automatic requirement for change; we can and do live with inconsistencies. But identity is, by nature, a presentational aspect of our selves. We are usually prepared to display in language what we hold inside.

Campaigns are also interesting because of the personal associations they encourage. A national campaign awash in heavy television news coverage is an invitation to see one's views and fantasies enacted by a celebrated agent, often in a form of hypercompression and narration that makes the campaign generically almost indistinguishable from other forms of entertainment. Candidates who generate a certain degree of passion are more than the sum of their "positions on the issues." They are also vessels to contain aspects of our own identity.[55] Through a kind of melded surrogacy, attacks on them are attacks on ourselves. Unique aspects of their biography may replicate parallels in our own. And their victories or defeats become ours, especially when the campaign has been waged in the simplified codes of gender, race, and ethnicity.

Thus, identification and identity are linked in significant if unstable ways. Ideas reflected in analogical reframing or ideological renaming have real consequences. The importance of identification to the communication process lies in its power to alter the relationships we have to the rest of our world. What we recognize almost immediately in the attitudes of converts and passionate believers in all realms of life is their sense of explicit connection to a person, a group, or a vocabulary.

The remaining sections of this chapter briefly explore two very different but intriguing questions left unresolved by our understanding of these processes. First, if identification presumes recognition of aspects of the self in others—or in other ideas—how do we accept identification's presumption of the "static" self against the modernist view that we are infinitely adaptive and other-directed? In other words, are we attempting to identify a process that is too fixed to account for the fact that identity is dynamic and constantly changing? Second, labeling the process of identification seems much easier than refining our understanding of its intensity. Do we have any functional schemes for estimating the strength of associations? Both questions resurface in the remaining chapters, but they are relevant here in indicating where we need to go in building on the Burkean model.

The Constructed Self: Reversing the Identity Arrows

When we think of identification in its most basic form (i.e., "She shares my views"), our conceptual model is often of a segment of discourse that fits with a preexisting attitude. Through this process, we often say that a person has "connected," "empathized," and so on. The assumption we make is that identification is a course traveled by our consciousness where we seek matches between our selves and external ideas and events. In this view our consciousness resembles a partly completed puzzle. The varied aspects of identity are relatively fixed; they have a particular shape that requires a complementary fit. Some ideas and appeals leave us unaffected because we do not have an affinity for them. Others "connect" and interlock with the rest of who we are. The analogy of a magnet offers parallel notions of a permanent self in search of complementary externals. The magnets of our dispositions are polarized, predisposed to attract or repel, and at other times completely indifferent to the nonferrous realm of experiences that mean nothing to us. The "knack" of rhetorical invention thus rests on discovering an individual's realm of acceptance where ideas offered are likely to be accepted as the individual's own.

Neither analogy should be taken very far, but their common feature of "finding an appropriate fit" nicely parallels the conventional view that humans are owners of relatively stable identities. The evidence for prior experience as a static frame of reference for new experience is substantial. And the human preference for constancy over change is overwhelming. But all of these come with an important caveat: identity is more fluid than we might assume.

Our mistake is that we think of identity as a collection of attributes: a set of unchanging properties. But however useful the concept is as a heuristic convenience, the deeper nature of identity suggests a very fluid state that defies easy predictions about what will produce successful identification and attraction. Gordon Allport called this the "dilemma of uniqueness":

> Personality is less a finished product than a transitive process. While it has some stable features, it is at the same time continually undergoing change. . . . Each person is an idiom unto himself, an apparent violation of the syntax of the species.[56]

Allport's point was to caution his colleagues that the pattern of the biological sciences to ignore the individuality within a species comes at too high a price if it carries over to human behavior.

David Riesman's description of what he called "other direction" also provides an essential reminder of the perils of assuming the existence of a fixed identity. Using language that has now entered into widespread use, Riesman has argued that modern society rewards members who place greater value on "responsive contact" with others rather than with those who have a firmly internalized sense of self. "Other-direction" as a defining feature of character keeps a larger range of attitudes and personal choices in play. For the other-directed person identity is less a matter of personal consistency then a response to the exigencies of the moment. Where the "inner-directed" person may form a relatively stable set of beliefs and values, the other-directed individual is willing to negotiate them, as social demands require. We reward such flexibility, while questioning behavior that flows from a rigid set of core beliefs. The person "out of step with the times" may be thought of as a social isolate, someone who is "rigid," "inflexible," "not a team player," and so on. "While the inner-directed person could be 'at home abroad' by virtue of his relative insensitivity to others," notes Riesman, "the other-directed person is, in a sense, at home everywhere and nowhere, capable of a rapid if sometimes superficial intimacy with . . . everyone."[57] For this person "life is a big pinball game and you have to be able to move and adjust yourself to situations if you're going to enjoy it. You got to realize that most things are not absolute."[58] Other direction feeds the impulse for identification, for "fitting in."

Riesman's language is interesting because it implies a quandary that is relevant to our concerns; namely, how does one identify with another agent who has an infinitely adjustable self? We often attribute persuasive advocates (i.e., politicians) with other direction. In the conventional stereotype, some are like the title character in Woody Allen's film *Zelig*. They will say anything or become anyone in order to fit in. Indeed, we expect effective advocates in the business of finding clients or votes to be other-directed. Sales and politics are often portrayed as activities populated by rudderless and shallow men,[59] always "on the make" and always ready to find a social opening that allows them to link their identity to others. But if the arrows are reversed and the intended audience for a message is a vessel that is more empty than full, identification in any profound sense seems less possible. To be meaningful as a concept, identification needs audiences that have a sense of who they are and that know which of their experiences and values really matter. Such individuals have a sense of their own distinctiveness, a set of convictions about themselves and their "place" in the world.[60]

I raise this not to create a psychology of identification, which would divert us from our emphasis on rhetorical acts, but to note that we cannot be too certain in predicting how appeals will play out on others. If Riesman and others such as Erving Goffman, Christopher Lasch, and Joshua Meyrowitz are correct,[61] the nature of the American character has subtly but significantly shifted in the last century. We now measure our lives less in terms of sets of core values and beliefs, and more in terms of our abilities to adjust to the social demands placed on us in a culture that prizes adaptation to a pluralistic world. Our reference points for identity have moved from the internal to the external. Correspondingly, we are more open to the value of accommodating attitudes very different from our own. *And we may now be less addressable in terms of a limited number of salient commitments and experiences.*

The Difficulty in Labeling Intensity

Notwithstanding the problems associated with a "static" view of identity, it is surprising we have so few constructs that allow us to characterize levels of intensity for identifications. Perhaps because meaning and significance are so variable within individuals, we do not have the equivalent of a seismic scale that gives more exactitude to estimates of the saliency of a given linkage. This imprecision contributes to what Wendell Harris calls the "terminological promiscuity" of most criticism.[62]

That identification remains descriptively impoverished is unusual, given its centrality as an emotional link between text and audience. Drama is constructed to let us see the importance of these connections; and the memoir gives a fluent author the forum to explain elaborate chains of unique associations. But the critic must describe every event anew, without recourse to a vocabulary that could be a common medium of exchange in making estimates of intensity. The problem is not that we lack a set of operational terms that would replace ordinary qualitative language. The difficulty is more basic; we lack even a qualitative language of degrees. The analysis of language and its functions often seems to be in *binary* rather than *graded* terms. Hence we talk about language that is expressive and instrumental, connotative and denotative, literal and figurative, and so on. But in interpreting the process of identification, we often rely on evocative but nonspecific terms that suggest the experience at the high end of the continuum: language that captures moments when identification yields a deep sense of connection (i.e., "catharsis," "peak experience," "deep understanding," "ecstasy," etc.).

It is beyond my goal to unilaterally proscribe a quick remedy that would instantly enrich a terminological desert. In any case, without anchors in a larger theoretical or methodological scheme, such arbitrary language would be useless. The real difficulty is how to characterize gradations of intensity that individuals or audiences attach to the presentation of a specific element in a message. The significance of a given text will always be subject to the experiences and influences that have played out in their lives. As Harris notes,

> The very nature of commentary on literature guarantees that a text of any interest will allow the assignment of multiple significances: one might well define the degree of potential interest of a text in terms of the extent to which it lends itself to the production of significances.[63]

What we need is an enriched language of description that offers a continuum of potentially involving evocations of empathy. It often takes the descriptive gifts of a writer to allow us to see how one person or event can create *collective* significance, changing a nation's consciousness and enhancing its sense of connection to an event or a person. Archibald MacLeish's famous tribute to broadcaster Edward R. Murrow and his chilling wartime broadcasts from London is a case in point. More than any other reporter, Murrow paved the way for acceptance of the inevitability of the American participation:

> You burned the city of London in our houses and we felt the flames that burned it. You laid the dead of London at our doors and we knew the dead were our dead—were all men's dead—were mankind's dead. . . .[64]

Murrow's place is nicely communicated in MacLeish's links between "you," "we," and "our." Murrow created powerful associations that made the war "ours," even before we officially entered it.

His resonant baritone became a trusted carrier of its meaning. Macleish's assessment is partly "poetic," and ought to be understood on its own terms. But it is also a description of one broadcaster's importance as a rhetorical agent capable of producing a collective consciousness, and as such, fits unclearly at the top end of a continuum of identification experiences.

My partial solution to this problem is to look to film criticism for an enriched vocabulary of *graded* effects. In various ways that will be explored in the next chapter, film theory offers a reminder similar to MacLeish's: that ideas carried by sympathetic characters are likely to enhance the potency of a message. The language of dramatic effects is a useful way to supplement our general understanding of identification.

To Sum Up: Defining Features of the Rhetorical Perspective

From the rhetorical and sociological frames of reference used here and the previous chapter, individuals can be viewed as the products of a "negotiated settlement" with cultural forces that have linked language with experience. A crucial role is exerted by audiences outside of the self, in the communities that we take as our own. We know these audiences must be addressed in ways they will accept. And we are often prepared to incorporate pieces of their world into our own.

Language, learning, and identification are intimately related. Learning is always a dialogue between memory and interpretation. We use prior experience as a basis for interpreting new events. Children begin their long careers as learners, first coming to recognize their sensate world. These familiar features eventually become the elements of their "known" universe in a process that expands and repeats itself over a lifetime. The ability to identify the familiar plays out first in the physical world of things, and within one year—the onset of language—begins to include a second world of representational constructs. With the transition out of early childhood, the dominance of the sociorhetorical environment takes on an importance that begins to dwarf the physical. Self is increasingly defined in terms of the expectations and acceptance of others. Signs yield to symbols as purveyors of meaning and significance. And "living in the present" gives way to increasing interest in living through the narratives of history, fiction, and the newsworthy events of contemporary life.

So we begin life with a memory that converts experience into meaning. If we are lucky, we reach the end of our days still holding on to many of these acquisitions, interpreting and reinterpreting their significance. In the process of transforming an event "known" to have a certain stipulated meaning to an event to which we have assigned an increased importance, we convert certain experiences into valuable personal assets.

When I was a five- or six-year old, I was first given a 78-rpm record of cowboy actor Gene Autry singing "Rudolph the Red-Nosed Raindeer." At first, the record was simply another new possession. But cowboy heroes were not easily ignored by young boys in the Eisenhower years, even when they were singing songs that had nothing to do with Indians and horses. After a succession of endless Colorado winters, its once shinny grooves had been worn dull, even while its tune became etched in the mind. Music has a way of insinuating its eight-bar formulas into the brain. As an object, the old black record with its red "Columbia" label is gone. It was easily abandoned in the rush to gain a foothold in adolescence. But to hear this old recording today is to momentarily recapture a period, a place, and a memory tightly packed with details.

This delivers us again to the recurring features that characterize identification in its rhetorical sense. It is a heightened form of meaning attached to a moment of experience. Identification allows us to see a piece of ourselves in others, or in their representations. The generative sources for this effect can be enormously varied, ranging from the rhetoric of narrative and oratory, to the representational worlds of art and music. In all of these forms—as Kenneth Burke has noted—appeals can flow from conventional associations, evocative analogies, and accepted ideologies. He also noted that they can produce a range of rhetorical effects—some conscious, some not—including feelings of unity, as well as feelings of collective enmity toward others. And at their most subtle and subversive, identifications serve the social or political needs of one faction by using language that conceals the gaps between two very different worlds.

A significant identification is not necessarily an exact replication of who we "are" or what we believe, but is also a projection of a piece of the external world into our own, with a strong sense that the "fit" is appropriate. We may know it from its form, as in the case of music. Or it may spring from meanings attached to specific images, ideas, or individuals.

While our attention in this chapter has been mostly on Burke's interest in shared ideas, our focus in the next chapter is on the *individual* as a vessel of familiar experience. Drama and politics are very different, but both allow us to look at how identification flows from the fact that we can become "objects to ourselves." Figures on the screen or in the theater of national politics edge us to empathy or anger. Their choices tempt comparison with our own. And, most importantly, the tools used for assessing our "relationships" with them can enrich our understanding of character-driven identifications.

Chapter 3

IDENTIFICATION, CELEBRITY, AND THE HOLLYWOOD FILM

We master it or appreciate it or enjoy it; it works, hits us hard, carries us away, absorbs or transports us. To me, as to Kenneth Burke, the most nearly adequate metaphors lead here to the notion of identification—I take the work in, or, as phenomenologists say, it enables me to dwell in it. I live in the work; it lives its life in me. Its creator and I become, in a part of our lives, indistinguishable as we live the work together.

—Wayne Booth, *Modern Dogma and the Rhetoric of Assent*

Poetry doesn't belong to those who write it, but to those who need it.

—Massimo Troisi, *Il Postino*

Virtually every form of narrative offers the potential to be a mirror of the self. In a process that sometimes defies simple explanations, we establish emotional connections with characters and circumstances that seem to mimic our own. The rewards of narrative include the chance to recognize the familiar in a new setting, and the opportunity to see some of the conditions of our own lives acted upon by others. Storytelling feeds on its own energy as a multiplier of experience. The richer intellectual and emotional life that it makes possible is its own reward. Aaron Copland—the composer-in-residence in these pages—has ironically noted that "not infrequently I have been moved to tears in the theater, [but] never at music." He seemed to envy drama's "naked" emotional power, all the more so if Bette Davis happened to have a starring role in a film.[1]

45

Arguably, no medium provides more opportunities for identification than film, with its ability to bypass the printed page and arrive to an audience with context and character in full expressive form. It is a cliché to note that film transports us to another place and, with it, another person's world. But as Bela Balazs has noted, the special capacity for identification is film's "absolute artistic novelty":

> Although we sit in our seats for which we have paid, we do not see Romeo and Juliet from there. We look up to Juliet's balcony with Romeo's eyes and look down on Romeo with Juliet's. Our eye and with it our consciousness is identified with the characters in the film, we look at the world out of their eyes and have no angle of vision of our own.[2]

In this chapter I will explore film's ability to construct this intense kind of consciousness. And like most analysts intrigued by its potency, I start with the same basic questions. Why does film draw us in so completely? Why do some film characters and the actors that create them become such powerful icons in popular culture? In the words of one writer, "Why do many of us fall in love so easily with characters onstage and in film?"[3]

In some ways the answers are no deep mystery. Film saturates the senses with information. A darkened theater intensifies film's impact and lets us step out of ourselves. No other medium so effortlessly transports us to another world or puts us in tighter proximity to memorable characters. In many other ways the appeal of film runs parallel with the attractions of narrative in general and fiction in particular.[4] Storytelling in all of its forms provides a mirror to ourselves and a window from which to view others.

Even so, there are significant differences between narratives on the page and those on the screen. Written narratives require effort, imagination and much more active intellectual engagement. The reader must be a more active participant in the process than a filmgoer. In addition, there are intriguing differences that surface in the notorious problems of converting novels into films. Written narratives can dwell on abstract ideas and thoughts. Their characters can more easily describe their doubts and inner feelings. And narrators can observe and comment at length, effortlessly moving between scenes and time frames. But both of these conventions of written exposition transfer awkwardly to film. With its natural orientation toward action and reaction, film requires its characters to do something. The subtleties and detours of written exposition are traded for the pleasures of living through another character.

This representational clarity primes us for identification: a fact that—more than any other—explains and feeds a continuing national obsession with the film industry's politics, economics, and especially its stars. It has been said that Americans have two different occupations: their own careers, and their impulse to keep up with the celebrity machine of Hollywood. The industry needs and feeds a constant national appetite for tracking the successes and failures of stars we have come to "know." It also supports thousands of professional journalists and academics by providing a ceaseless stream of content to analyze, mostly from the starting assumption that film is especially persuasive in the ways it legitimizes and distributes power.

For all of these reasons film remains a special case. For many of us, it *perfects* the dramaturgy of novel and the play, improving on the apparatus of discursive writing and the fixed perspective of the theater. At the same time, it *perfects* moments in a life, offering portraits of individuals "like us" or like others we can imagine: characters who have often been created to literally "flesh out" an expected melodramatic *ethos.* The first part of this chapter explores the nature of this process, and a terminology for describing it. And because stardom feeds what sometimes amounts to an ongoing "relationship" between actors and audiences, I will also touch on the relationship between celebrity and identification. Celebrity has interesting parallels in the worlds of film and national politics. The second part of this chapter builds on the premise that some models and methods of film analysis have value in accounting for the generative power of character in many forms of public life.

A Methodological Minefield

Every ideology offers interpreters of films and their significant agents as carriers of meaning compelling portraiture. One can approach identification as a Freudian,[5] Marxist, or feminist.[6] The high church of identification theory sometimes takes its analytic framework from psychoanalysis, which sees film identification in parallel terms to dreams and fantasy construction. In the deterministic language of this system, film viewing provokes comparison with the evolving ego, and feeds into unconscious processes of identity formation.[7] But the effects of characters on audiences are sometimes more transitory, and more clearly the product of recent experience than a long evolutionary history. Applying the psychoanalytic framework to specific films can be like trying to drive a 60s-vintage Cadillac through the narrow streets of Rome. Leaving the Italian capital years ago, I remember seeing one of these massive land yachts heading the other way. It had been lovingly cared after by its owner, an American in a military uniform. But an old Cadillac is a bloated alien in that crowded cityscape, and certainly not nimble enough to handle the old byways and the modern traffic.[8]

A practical theory of film identification similarly needs less weight if is to be able to account for its evanescent effects. The approach taken here is more structural than ideological, and more attentive to the fundamental mechanisms of cinematic narrative that work to increase or decrease the capacity for identification. It includes how knowledge is "apportioned" about characters, and how "point of view"—an especially salient feature of the medium—primes audiences to identify with some characters and not others.

Film Narrative and Identification

Jackie Stacey's survey of women's responses to Hollywood stars from the 1940s and 1950s is revealing. Immediately After World War II, film still dominated popular entertainment in the United States and much of Europe. Bette Davis, Deanna Durbin, Katharine Hepburn and others clearly became objects of devotion and imitation, carriers of on-screen personas that could be projected into one's own life. In Stacey's surveys of British women, film characters produced different but related effects expressed in the language of emulation: pretending, resembling, imitating and copying.[9] "I loved to watch Deanna Durbin," noted one. "I used to put myself in her place. She lived in a typical girl's dream." Another woman recalls seeing her future in the conscious emulation of Rita Hayworth. "I always imagined, if I could look like her I could toss my red hair into the wind ... and meet the man of my dreams."[10] A third remembers a fixation on Doris Day:

I wanted to write and tell of you my devotion to my favourite star Doris Day. I thought she was fantastic, and joined her fan club, collected all the photos and info I could. I saw *Calamity Jane* 45 times in a fortnight and still watch her films avidly. My sisters all thought I was mad going silly on a woman, but I just thought she was wonderful, they were mad about Elvis, but my devotion was to Doris Day.[11]

What is sometimes called "wishful identification" flows from the desire to idolize or be like someone else.[12] It always seems to be present in the lives of young children, but extends well beyond early life to become a constant for the most attentive of film viewers. The record-setting audience for the 1998 film *Titanic* is a reminder of this common process. By all accounts it was not the film's elaborate special effects that drew almost half of its young women viewers back for a second or third look, but its teen love story.[13] A large number had clearly invested a piece of themselves in the fate of the love-struck couple and the high-visibility stars who played them.

The gravitational pull that portraits of heroes have on audiences can take several forms. Building on the literary aesthetics of Hans Jauss,[14] P. David Marshall offers four complementary "modalities of reception." Each reflects a slightly different entry point for establishing a connection with the consumer of a narrative.

1. *Associative identification*: The barriers between audience and actors are broken and there is a celebration of active participation.

2. *Admiring identification*: The actions of the hero are exemplary for a particular community—the perfect hero.

3. *Sympathetic identification*: There is a solidarity with the character or suffering personality. We place ourselves in the position of the hero.

4. *Cathartic identification*: [A] moral judgment can be drawn from the aesthetic experience and the reader feels a sense of emancipation through his or her involvement with the character.[15]

As a practical matter, and if we had the means to track specific responses, all of these forms would clearly overlap. And while all offer the same root effect of binding us to the fate hero, each is a point on an increasing scale of intensity. Associative identification, for example, speaks to the essential task of the communicator to engage an audience: to bring them into a story and make them care about the unfolding drama. At the other extreme, cathartic identification suggests that characters may provide individuals with models for some form of personal transformative change: perhaps the most potent effect strong identifications can produce.[16]

Following a similar pattern of progressively involving levels of identification, Murray Smith has described three distinct levels of "imaginative engagement with characters"—recognition, alignment, and allegiance—which make a great deal of intuitive sense.[17] The terms represent a full "structure of sympathy" that ranges from simple "engagement"—what Smith describes as a weak form of identification—to the emotionally more potent level of "allegiance." Like the Jauss/Marshall scheme, the value of Smith's descriptive language lies in its ability to offer graded distinctions that separate simple forms of recognition from higher forms of identification where an individual acts *as the carrier of the spectator's sensibilities.*

The first level of "recognition" accounts for "the spectator's construction of character" based on collection of actions and attitudes specified by the narrative. We "read" the actions and intentions of others from the perspective of our own relevant past experience. And "we assume that these traits correspond to analogical ones we find in persons in the real world."[18] We may not fully identify with particular agents, but we draw from our own experience to understand their acts and apparent motivations. Recognition requires only "that the spectator understand that these traits and mental states make up the character."[19]

Consider Charlie Chaplin's invention of the tramp, a character that was nearly synonymous with his career. With the possible exception of Groucho Marx, no film icon so successfully fed the American appetite to skewer the pretensions of wealth and official authority. The tramp was both larger and smaller than life: less a fully rounded character than the embodiment of certain wistful values (earnestness, gentleness, playfulness, etc.). We identify less with him than the circumstances in which he has been placed. In the many films that featured the character, Chaplin's figure was tossed into a larger hostile malevolent world populated by wealthy

snobs, suspicious police, and heartless bosses. This mix of characters was easy for earlier audiences to recognize in terms of the hard
economic times of the period. In films such as *Modern Times* they
were usually "read" as dark villains, in sharp contrast to the mixture of innocence and beauty represented by the tramp and Paulette
Goddard's "gamin." Audiences didn't literally want to be like the
tramp. The films got their humor and edge because they could
recognize the malevolent forces working against him.

The second level of *alignment* is based on how a script and
the camera apportions knowledge about characters. Film privileges
some agents by giving them an emotional life and a past that allows
us to interpret their actions. Others are denied these humanizing
details. Knowledge is apportioned in a variety of ways: in the use
of reaction shots that force us to absorb the full weight of a person's
emotions, in interior monologues that allow us to eavesdrop on
their thoughts, and especially in the interactions and general plot
devices that reveal personal attributes and qualities that we are
supposed to respect or reject. In small and large ways we are set up
to take the measure of agents in the closely observed ways they
respond to events. As publisher Michael Korda has noted, most
editors have to remind inexperienced novelists to "show rather
than tell."[20] Scenes with character-revealing dialogue are usually
more interesting to audiences than straight narration.

Smith notes that alignment does not require that the spectator
"replicate the thoughts or emotions of the character."[21] But the
generous apportionment of time or point of view with a character
naturally increases the chances for empathy. And, indeed, the very
meaning of alignment implies the convergence of a character's perspective with an audience's. For example, Hollywood film conventions that govern how we learn about a character's death have the
certainty of a sunrise. A person who momentarily struggles with
blurred vision or a cough in the first half-hour is almost guaranteed
to be dead by the third act. And a movie that opens with a major
star and an unknown as a married couple telegraphs the news that
the star's character will soon be a widower. The rules that govern
the deaths of heroes and villains are equally predictable.

In the 2001 film *Pearl Harbor*, for example, we see the Japanese attack in Honolulu from the perspective of the stunned and
frightened Americans around the naval base. The camera dwells on

the violence of the assault, in one case showing the outstretched arms of doomed sailors who cannot be saved by their comrades just a few feet away. But an American bombing attack on Tokyo shown later in the film is shot entirely from the perspective of the bombers. A safe distance from the chaos on the ground denies us similar alignment with the Japanese. Likewise, in the pre-feature matinee serials of my youth (25 cents then bought an afternoon of mayhem and revenge), western bad guys and many Indians were dispatched by being shot on camera, but left to die out of its range. An extended and painful demise was the prerogative of a hero or a victim. Good guys died in close-up, bringing the audience into the pathos of the scene.

Thirdly, Smith notes that the most potent form of emotional engagement is generated at the level of "*allegiance*," a process where a character is seen as the principled anchor of the action.[22] A central canon of nearly all popular story telling requires certain figures to become vessels for the moral point of the story. These figures may be the agents of justice, fairness, decency, retribution, and many other responses. They are also our agents by proxy, carrying out acts that vindicate the problem or conflict that sits at the center of the story. As Smith notes,

> Allegiance depends upon the spectator having what s/he takes to be reliable access to the character's state of mind, understanding the context of the character's action, and having morally evaluated the character on the basis of this knowledge. . . . On the basis of such evaluations, spectators construct *moral structures*, in which characters are organized and ranked in a system of preference.[23]

This clearly gets us to the heart of the identification process in film. The medium is inherently persuasive in its power to control the flow and sequencing of information to maximize our understanding of a character's virtue. *Thelma and Louise* resonates mostly as an empowerment fable because the two title characters are the agents of just retribution against a series of misogynistic men. The slights and outrages inflicted on these working-class women made them potent surrogates for some audiences.[24]

It is not surprising that popular favorites often feature characters as objects of allegiance. Consider some of the Academy Award winners for "best picture" over the years. They include *Rocky* (1976), *Kramer vs. Kramer* (1979), *Gandhi* (1982), *Terms of Endearment* (1983), *Driving Miss Daisy* (1989), *Shakespeare in Love* (1998), and *A Beautiful Mind (2001).* Each film guaranteed its popular acceptance by giving audience members a stake in the triumph of at least one character over significant adversity. They all asked for the audience to commit to the decency of its central protagonist. To overlay Marshall's terms at this level of allegiance, the suffering portrayed in *Gandhi* is transcendent and potentially cathartic. In the domestic settings portrayed in *A Beautiful Mind* and *Kramer vs. Kramer* the identifications are probably better described as existing in the realm of the "sympathetic" or "admiring."

If allegiance is not an automatic guarantor of commercial success, it certainly represents a potent Hollywood convention. Narratives that violate this expectation often leave audiences uncertain about where to invest the emotional energy they are primed to give. The recent film, *A.I.: Artificial Intelligence,* offers such a case of problematic allegiance. The Stanley Kubrick/Steven Spielberg project portrays a future that has produced a class of super robots that can stand in as surrogates for real people, including children. It asks us to keep some emotional distance from Haley Joel Osment's beguiling portrayal of "David," a experimental and lifelike child robot that has been irrevocably imprinted with the need to seek the love of a "mother" whose real son remains in an extended coma. In the film the humans are cruel and opportunistic, while the robots have been programmed to be idealized versions of their human counterparts. Slowly and irrevocably it steers its audience into an emotional box with no easy exit. The loving David is the irresistible center of the story; all the more so because he has been abandoned by his "family" and begins a terrifying journey to rejoin his "mother." David's quest easily becomes the audience's as well. But David is a machine who will easily outlive the "mother" he has been programmed to find. He cannot change. And Spielberg's decision to cast a real child instead of a machine creates an audience bond that reflects his own affinities for storytelling from a child's point of view. It is little wonder that audiences found its inconclusive third act unsettling. Can one identify with a machine? Can the audience deny Osment's flesh and feelings? Identification as allegiance is a powerful form of attraction. If we succumb to the charms of "David," we are left to live through the tragic and unsettling experiences of a gentle 11-year-old boy.

Narrative Distance and Identification

The postmodern impulse in most art is to skewer the idea of an idealized hero by denying him sole possession of the moral high ground. Referring again to the work of Jauss, P. David Marshall notes the popular aphorism that "great works emerge from a break with the horizon of expectation." In "high" literature or innovative cinema "there is maintenance of the interaction with the audience without a sense of the closure of character identification."[25] In this ironic modality, as Jauss notes, "an expectable identification is held out to the spectator or reader only to be subsequently refused or ironized."[26] Familiar narrative conventions are violated or ignored, and heroes instead become antiheroes or allegorical figures. These shifts open up some "distance" between the audience and the characters. In the words of Bertolt Brecht, characters become objects of our "inquiry" rather than people who ask us to "share" their "experience."[27]

How far can a story drift from the center of expectations before it begins to sacrifice it chances to establish agents that we still care about? The short answer seems to be "quite a lot," but it must be noted that identifications are not quite as easy to assess in narratives that aspire more to artistic rather than commercial values. The differences between the two are easily oversimplified, but they serve as useful guides for exploring narrative distance.

Peter Wollen seems to have this distinction in mind in his description of "counter cinema," where there is a greater allegiance to "art" rather than commerce, and there is a greater willingness to develop narratives that favor ambiguity over sentimentalized closure.[28] In the conventional view of this divide, commercial films are shown in suburban multiplexes; independent films are seen at festivals and university film series. And of course studio films produce revenue; the work of independents tends to produce less cash and more "buzz." Most importantly, "commercial" films are far more likely to align heroes with existing expectations: content to make characters at "the moral center" who will not disappoint. Leonardo DiCapario is said to have protested to director James Cameron that his character in *Titanic* existed without a dark side.[29] Fair enough. But the young man who boarded the doomed ship was there in part to keep the commercial value of the narrative afloat: to let his simple goodness "play" against the stuffy formality of the ship's first-class passengers.[30]

The ironic modality of "independent" or counter-cinema is reflected in Simon Moore's and Stephen Gaghan's script for the film *Traffic*. Released in 2000, the three-part story masterfully explores the failings and faulty assumptions of the "drug war," with its emphasis on police-state tactics to control supply rather than the heavy demand for drugs by millions of Americans. "Traffic" presents even its ostensibly law-abiding characters—American and Mexican drug police, a new White House "drug czar" and others— as both victims of the "war" and unintended servants to the needs of some part of the drug industry. Because it dramatizes the background of corruption and compromise that lurks just behind official declarations of successful drug interdiction, it leaves us to observe the lives of its major characters with a greater sense of ambivalence.

Traffic shares a postmodern documentary style with many other contemporary films. It creates imperfect people in an imperfect world. And, in a simplistic sense, it reflects one side in a medium that seems to have its own bipolar nature.

Although the line between the two has blurred in recent years, this broad distinction between commercial and independent films is still useful because of the ideological split it represents. The independent side of the industry tends to view easy identifications with suspicion. Hollywood takes a good deal of criticism for making narrative choices that guarantee "safe" one-dimensional roles. Characters created primarily to sell tickets and maximize revenue are likely to be too restrictive and too prone to rely on outdated identities.[31] Simplified heroes and villains, for example, can feed old and outmoded stereotypes, in addition to serving as vehicles of a hegemonic social agenda that resists change. In the commercial model, characters are "products." They function like commodities that have been refined through the use of "Q" ratings, questionnaires, and focus groups.[32] Given the lag time between social innovation and social change, the result can be the "design" of characters that still successfully pander to yesterday's values. In the financially successful film *Pretty Woman*, for example, we get several of these values in one character: the prostitute with a "heart of gold," a woman whose new identity is defined by her rich companion, and a rising actress (Julia Roberts) whose beauty is partly used to "carry" the film.

In addition, any postmodern "take" on narrative also needs to account for our undeniable attraction to flawed characters and anti-heroes. Even if they look far different from the sentimental figures of earlier decades played by actors like John Wayne or Henry Fonda, they still have their uses. As the classification schemes of both Marshall and Murray suggest, there are a variety of ways to engage the viewer or reader in the lives of pivotal characters. There is ample room to find similarity, for example, at the "associative" level described by Jauss and Marshall, and the "recognition" level offered by Murray. In the portraits of "weak" figures that have left a trail of failures over the course of three acts, we can still find sufficient evidence to "relate."

Just how elastic our sympathies can be is seen in our identification with down-on-their luck drifters that represent entrepreneurial America's untouchables. "Ratso" and Joe in John Schlesinger's *Midnight Cowboy* are naïve and sometimes malevolent, but ultimately endearing. The narrative distance between our lives and their's is enormous. We've seen them on 42nd Street, when it was still the gritty midtown New York neighborhood of hustlers and tourists. Their hopes are pathetic, but at the same time recognizable in their hustle and optimism. Kenneth Lonergan's more recent *You Can Count on Me* offers another portrayal of a drifter: a hapless brother approaching middle age who passes through the life of his concerned sister. She still lives in the upstate New York home that became theirs after their parents died, managing to piece together her work in a bank with the responsibilities of single parenthood. But Terry reappears out of the blue to put new fractures in a life that was beginning to feel comfortable. It is clear that he is still purposeless, and that she may be the only person to provide an anchor. All the same, he is no less compelling for his failings. We don't want to be Terry, but Lonergan has made it easy for audiences to do what Smith described at his first level: to recognize the familiar outlines of a life that has stalled just short of maturity. Neither character is constructed to ask for our total empathy. But both at least invite our understanding.

These very different films suggest the need for a more nuanced view of identification that reaches beyond the idea of similarity.

Identification clearly includes the capacity to see a part of ourselves—our thoughts, actions, and fantasies—in the very human
but less-than-ideal circumstances of others. As Hugh Duncan has
noted, drama is rooted in our sociality. It comments on our failings
as well as our fantasies. And it serves much of the same function
as journalism.[33] With their implicit considerations of motives and
choices, and even when there is a considerable difference between
the circumstances of the characters and those of the audience, nearly
all narratives of fact or fiction provide potential connections.

Identification and Point of View

Imagine that a film director is about to shoot a scene that
involves a character returning to her home that has been ransacked
by an unknown intruder. Without getting into further plot details,
it is easy to see that how the scene is presented will greatly effect
the audience's reaction toward the character. If the camera stays on
the side of the door with the actor, we see the disheveled home as
she does. The story at that moment is told from her point of view.
But if the director instead places the camera on the inside of the
room as the same sequence begins, we see the scene unfold as a
separate observer. In this case we know more than the character,
and our interest is going to be focused on her reaction.

With either decision we may still empathize with her. But, all
things being equal, the choice to disclose information as the character sees it will tend to align the audience with her. By contrast,
the second scenario that gives us knowledge of what has already
happened creates more distance. In that single moment we are no
longer "participants" in the actions of her life; we have instead
become distanced observers of it.

In film, point of view is generally thought of as having two
dimensions: the narrative and visual. The first constructs a psychological and structural frame of reference. It primes us to accept the
motives and actions of some while rejecting others. The second is the
same as our example: the sum total of all the camera shots that tend
to align with a sympathetic character. In either case, information and
empathy is apportioned to some characters and denied to others. In
actual practice, even the most formulaic films will sometimes change
point of view as the needs of the story require.[34] But this basic principle of throwing an audience's alignment and allegiance to some

agents and denying it to others is a central process for identification. It's interesting to see how the process works in what has become "Exhibit A" in the analysis of narrative perspective.

In most of Alfred Hitchcock's films the camera apportions knowledge to force audiences into the uncomfortable position of knowing too little about the risks they face. Among others, *Psycho* and *Vertigo* come to mind as stories told almost exclusively through the eyes of their troubled victims. But *Rear Window* stacks the deck even more. In this film not only is the story told visually from the point of view of its sympathetic victims, but the narration also apportions knowledge to (in Smith's scheme) *align* us with them, and then—ultimately—to ask for our *allegiance* as well.

Hitchcock's 1954 classic created a self-contained world that could be observed from the window of "Jeff" Jefferies's Greenwich Village apartment. Stewart's character is a restless photographer who has taken assignments in the most remote corners of the world. He is used to roughing it in his quests for the perfect photo of an alien landscape. But a broken leg has left him restricted to a small New York studio facing onto other apartments that share a small interior courtyard. Restless and bored, he passes the time by observing the sights and sounds that spill out of his neighbors' windows. And before long, his obsession with the private stories that go with these evocative fragments begins to take hold.

This is, of course, *Rear Window's* famous motif. We are all voyeurs, and perhaps never more so than as film viewers. Hitchock's story simply makes the metaphor literal. Our impulse to be spectators is a reminder of how easily we are drawn into the action that takes place behind the missing fourth wall.

As most critics note, the story unfolds from Jeffries's frame of reference.[35] In Laura Mulvey's phrase, the story is "cut to the measure of (male) desire."[36] And the object of his and the camera's gaze is clearly Grace Kelly's elegant and smart Lisa Fremont.[37] The Park Avenue socialite obviously adores Jeff and visits him everyday with the apparent aim of wearing down his opposition to a life together in New York. Their relationship is at a stalemate. She wants to stay in the city, he is itching to return to the open spaces of distant continents. Lisa is also bothered by Jeff's inattention to her, and his increasing fascination with the unfolding dramas of his backyard theater.

There is a woman Jeffries calls "Miss Lonelyhearts," who sometimes sets her dinner table for companions that do not come. The pathos of her sad fantasies momentarily awaken Lisa and Jeff to the invasiveness of their attention. There is also a musician in the fifth-floor terrace apartment to the right who moves from elation to drunken despair in the space of a single evening. His glass-walled aerie is as transparent as his theatrical mood swings. And, of course, there is the centerpiece of the story in the second-floor apartment directly across the small courtyard: the troublesome puzzle of the brooding salesman and his invalid wife.

What Jeff has exactly seen and heard is unclear. In a brilliant application of point of view through sound, we hear him in barely audible conversations that ricochet off the courtyard's walls. The conversations that drift across the open space between the buildings are blurred, but there are moments when the bed-bound wife seems to alternatively nag and mock the unhappy husband. Several days later, when her bed is suddenly empty and the salesman appears to be cleaning up knives and saws in the kitchen sink, Jeff is sure a murder has occurred. He places a call to the salesman to get him out of the apartment so Lisa can go investigate: a risky move that will briefly land her in jail.

Not a frame of film is wasted in emotionally tying us to the fate of these two characters.[38] The exposition of their early scenes together is intended to make us care. We want them to work out their differences. In the real world it would hard to imagine any film characters less suited for a life together. She is in her element in New York; he clearly is not. But Grace Kelly and Jimmy Stewart are compulsively watchable and likable, the ineffable combination of their own stardom and good screenwriting. Add in the context of the 1950s, and they are meant get married and share the same future. Lisa's spunk in gamely climbing over the murderer's balcony and into his apartment tells us everything we need to know. Even if she is dressed in an outfit more appropriate for a *Vogue* cover than for sleuthing, she's got what it takes to be Jeff Jefferies's partner.

By keeping the camera in the apartment throughout nearly all of *Rear Window*, Hitchcock usually allows us to see and hear only what is also known to the couple. The film invites us to share their confusion and uncertainty. By contrast, the suspect is seen at a

distance that emphasizes his threatening persona. In what is arguably the film's best moment, Hitchcock reduces his villain to a
perfect image of hidden danger. Through Jeffries's open window we
see across to the salesman's apartment. But against the black of the
darkened living room we can only make out the eerie glow of his
cigarette as he ponders his next move.

Conventional horror and mystery films clearly have a special
need to develop a coherent point of view. An audience that knows
too much is denied the mystery. Hitchcock's effective film finds the
right balance, making us first care about his characters, and then
setting them and us loose in familiar but still dangerous waters.

The 1998 film *Run Lola Run* offers a starkly different take on
how to organize a film's point of view. "Lola" is also about a young
couple confronted with life-threatening choices. But Tom Tykwer's
story of desperation moves us out of a comfortable apartment and
onto the streets of Berlin. In a perfect reflection of its postmodern
style, it makes us spectators rather than participants in the lives of
Lola and her hapless boyfriend, Manni. Manni needs money to pay
off some shady thugs and has phoned Lola to tell her she has only
twenty minutes to come up with it. If she does not show up, he will
walk across the street from the phone booth and rob a grocery store.
Her race against Manni's desperation and an incessant clock is retold
three times. Each recounting of the events leading up to the robbery
is different: the result of small delays that effect Lola's frantic dash
through the streets of the city.

In the film Tykwer flaunts his indifference to the conventions
of exposition. The characters barely have a past and a social context
for their present lives. And although Lola's distress and determination barely make her a figure of alignment, most of the energy of the
film is spent exploring the premise that life and death hang on the
luck of events we cannot plan for. After the first scenario has played
out, we have traveled "ahead" and seen one version of the future.
The last two remaining variations make us spectators for the small
but significant changes that happen because of serendipity and
chance. The repeat sequences unfold as if we had put another quarter
in a slot to replay the same game. The result carries its own rewards
in terms of the slightly altered details of each replay of Lola's frantic run, but the film distances us from the couple. Lola's helpless-

ness draws us in. But in the end, we care less about them than the hypnotic rhythm of the race.

Stardom: Recognition of a Fixed Identity

Screenwriter William Goldman's operational definition of a "star" is someone who can "open" a film, meaning that celebrity actors can draw crowds to a theater even if the movie is "a stiff."[39] Some industry observers have argued that their value as guarantors of a certain amount of box office activity is greatly overrated.[40] Even so, their presence is an important factor in estimating the importance of identification to film.

Because of their common tendency to play a fairly narrow range of roles around their core persona, stars offer a level of continuity that functions as a powerful "draw" to audiences. In the old jargon of the studios, stars were "bankable" and "unknowns" were not. The presence of certain actors on a bill guaranteed to give a film a level of *gravitas* or glamour. "Character" actors may thrive on a variety of very different roles and physical requirements, a fact that can make them nearly unrecognizable from one film project to the next. But stardom guarantees recognition. Though always a very small percentage of the "talent" side of the entertainment industry, they have been transformed by their celebrity into figures of widespread public attachment. In a closed loop that feeds on its own energy, the star-making apparatus of the studios and news media create levels of public recognition that require even more coverage.

The star system is the source of many of Hollywood's horror stories and legends. The standard tropes of celebrity journalism view them as either spoiled children or ruthless careerists. And their presence often constrains the creative possibilities for a screenplay, since their basic on-camera persona must usually be kept intact. Charlie Chaplin stepped out of the "tramp" character at his peril. Audiences were slow to accept him in roles that cast him as a villain.[41] Admitting slightly larger variations in their on-screen roles, the same has been true for stars as different as John Wayne, Harrison Ford, and Julia Roberts.

The process of writing a screenplay is instructive in assessing how stars influence stories. John Gregory Dunne and Joan Dideon were signed by a major studio to write a script based on Alanna Nash's well-researched biography of newscaster Jessica Savitch.[42] Savitch lived as she died. Her messy life of depression, drugs, and broken relationships ended in 1983 after a freak car accident in a restaurant parking lot. In many ways her world mirrored the pressures and problems inherent in local television news, with its preoccupation with appearance over substance, and entertainment over solid journalism. But after eight years of negotiations with the studio and a mind-numbing marathon of twenty-seven separate drafts, Dunne and Dideon ended up with a story that had drifted far from the original biography. As Dunne later noted, they stuck with the project more for the money than the art, and because they had long ago given up any illusions about the literary sanctity of a Hollywood screenplay. The studio demanded and got a story that was safe and suitable for its two leading stars, Robert Redford and Michelle Pfeiffer.[43]

In the final version of *Up Close and Personal* Pfeiffer's character would be given the "soft focus" treatment. She was naïve but not overtly aggressive. Her mentors were no longer the venal tabloid artists and complacent anchorpersons in the book. All were essentially replaced by Robert Redford's Warren Justice, a hard-headed former war correspondent who would teach her the rudiments of serious reporting. In the end, the characters were reconstructed to be loved rather than simply understood. Whatever narrative distance might have existed in a more authentic portrayal of the troubled television news celebrity was minimized in a script that assured the audience's allegiance to the stars and their characters.

Since stardom is nearly synonymous with a stable and generally ingratiating persona, it creates a natural locus of "connection" and recognition. The familiarity of celebrity makes possible a mediated kind of relationship described by Donald Horton and Richard Wohl as "parasocial interaction." The parasocial relationship partly duplicates the sense of intimate knowledge that comes from recurring interpersonal contact.[44] The interesting twist is that it is "created at a distance," through repeated exposure to the same media characters. "The conditions of response to the performer are analogous to those in a primary group. The most remote and illustrious men are met *as if* they were in the circle of one's peers."[45] We "know" them so well that if we meet them, our inclination is to address them on a first-name basis.

Arguably the most important function of the star system is this parasocial continuity. The star's "brand identity" can never be lost completely to a character. A familiar texture of mannerisms tells us they are the same predictable and attractive person.[46] This repetition narrows the distance between celebrities and their audiences. Each new appearance in character or as their "authentic" selves affirms the same general impression. It is little wonder that potent Identifications flow from the unusual bridge that stardom creates: a span that connects the public and the private, and forces us into issues relevant to the role of celebrity in the larger culture. If film is the natural venue of the celebrity-making process, it is by no means unique. The effects of this process can be seen in many other corners of American life.

From the Public to the Private: Celebrity and the Downward Transformation of Identification

Our fascination with celebrity has a long history,[47] and carries its own shadow history of how identification with public figures has changed. An unbroken line links the culture of celebrity today with famous men and women from our past, including figures as diverse as Henry Ward Beecher and Buffalo Bill. Beecher was a star of the lecture circuit, appearing around the nation over twelve hundred times between 1875 and 1887.[48] And Buffalo Bill's celebrity was a case study in self-promotion. After a series of novels published about his exploits, Buffalo Bill Cody's "Wild West Show" toured Europe and the United States for over twenty years. The show's appearance in a town was always preceded by the larger-than-life legends of Annie Oakley and Sitting Bull, who magnified its importance.[49]

This kind of mid twentieth century celebrity had a certain innocence to it. Until the decade after World War II, a national figure's persona was largely constructed from his or her public acts. It is an oversimplification, but through most of the decade following the war it was still largely unacceptable to trade on distinctly personal information about public figures. The press did not necessarily believe the ballyhoos of the press agents that generated interest in earlier political, literary, and popular entertainment figures. But—with notable exceptions—they usually excluded the more problematic aspects of a celebrity's private history in their own reporting. As Richard Sennett notes, there was a natural predisposition against "the involuntary disclosure of character" to others.[50] Prewar America was still a culture of heroes. There was less of an impulse to engage in the demystification of public acts: a process that now fuels the current appetite for irony and paradox.

By the middle of the tumultuous 1960s a handful of cultural traumas combined with a sudden landslide of shifting values to challenge the separation of the public from the private. The assassinations of JFK, Robert Kennedy, Martin Luther King, and Malcolm X had taken their tolls. A "credibility gap" between what political leaders said and what they did left millions of Americans in doubt about governmental intentions regarding civil rights and Vietnam. News reports from the field and government briefing rooms sometimes started with the presumption that government was a source of disinformation.[51] By 1968, the seams of the national fabric were stretched to the breaking point. Old separations between the public and the private were rejected or undermined by simmering animosities between whites and blacks, young and old, political idealists and pragmatists.

These cultural and political dislocations began to feed growing generational differences over the value of civil society in relation to the "deeper" person. In the values of the vaguely defined youth culture, the separation of one's formal public self from the private self was an alien process: the imposition of the organizational world on our freer nature. In the context of our own times these forces may not seem mutually exclusive, but in the midcentury ferment they were often represented in oppositional terms. As Todd Gitlin phrased it, one had to learn to "live for the moment, without guarantees, in a world that doesn't deliver."[52] These themes first took hold in the 1950s in the writings of Jack Kerouac, the films of James Dean, and even peons to the false public self like the hit song, "The Great Pretender."[53] But they emerged in the following decade as part of the vague discontents of the young. There were many reasons the new baby-boom generation was attracted to these ideas, but none was more important than the fact that they were different from their parent's more practical postwar concerns.

The equally vague antidote for these ills was partly in the idea of personal authenticity and its corollaries of confession and demystification.[54] A compartmentalized life separating home and work, the private from the public, made less sense. In the words of the Students for a Democratic Society, "The goal of man and society should be human independence: a concern not with image (or) popularity but with finding a meaning in life that is personally authentic."[55] The endorsement of candor and the acceptance of self became part of a mantra that was easier to chant than to "live," but it flourished first in the politics and music of young elites, and then edged more uneasily into the core of American life. By the 1970s the vulgarized remnants of these ideas found their way through the corporate Mixmaster, resulting in everything from "hip" ads for Volkswagen "Beetles" to a television show that reduced this American schism to a "Laugh In."

As is noted in more detail in chapter 6, this newer ethic that challenges the separation of the personal from the public has also challenged older notions of journalistic propriety. Fields of public life as diverse as sports, art, science, politics and film were effected. In Hollywood the line was first breached in the late 1950s when the old "top down" studio system faded away. The end of the studios also meant an end to exclusive contracts, and the information monopolies of the studio publicity departments that went with them. These corporate press offices had carefully meted out "information" and sought to reassure audiences of the decency of stars under contract. With the removal of that buffer, stars were on their own. And celebrity was beginning to carry a virus that could instantly turn lethal to its carriers.

Politics and film followed parallel paths. In the older pattern, journalists did not write about the drinking problems of members of Congress, or the homosexuality of actors who had built successful careers as leading men. The various personal demons that are now the staples of celebrity and historical biography were less visible. In politics especially, one's lifestyle choices (homosexuality, infidelity, actions as a college student, etc.) mattered less than one's performance as a public figure. In sharp contrast, just two generations later journalists would use the cover of an independent counsel's incessant probes as justification to reveal the intimate details of extramarital sex in the Clinton White House. Ostensibly, the interests of the newer ethic of "full disclosure" had been served.

In addition to all of the generational reasons cited above, the parallel development of television through the same period played a significant role in changing the boundaries of public discourse. It is the very essence of television to feed on our insatiable interest in the private self. The cliché is true: television is an "intimate medium." As Joshua Meyrowitz notes, the corollary in its coverage of "real" life is a ceaseless fascination with the "back regions" of public lives.

> The backstage exposure of our high-status performers dramatically changes the relative flow of social information. With respect to our national leaders, for example, we have essentially reversed the nonreciprocal flow of information that traditionally supported high status. Leaders once had easy access to others, but were able to control access to themselves. . . . Through television, "the people" now have more access to the personal expressive behaviors of leaders than leaders have to the personal behaviors of the people.[56]

Few public figures remained unaffected by television's intrusive gaze. Even in the early years of the medium, broadcast journalist Edward R. Murrow became much more famous for his interviews with celebrities in their home via television's *Person to Person*, than his groundbreaking documentaries on the same network.[57] That show offered a circumspect peek behind the curtain of celebrity, sometimes leaving the austere war correspondent at a loss for words as guests rhapsodized about the details of their domestic life.

There is nothing new in the idea that celebrity breeds gossip. Celebrities are, after all, one of the common denominators of a culture. Their marriages and appetites are especially a source of common exchange, another informational commodity sold to consumers along with news, weather, and sports. What is striking is the extent to which the most private details about celebrities are now available for public scrutiny, often without their consent. One can look at the reporting of figures as diverse as Richard Nixon, Marilyn Monroe, or tennis star Arthur Ashe and see the same disclosive processes. The release of the Oval Office conversations at the end of the Watergate Affair showed a sometimes mean-spirited president with a racist's tendency for ethnic invective. They made him seem pathetically shallow and insecure.[58] And the exposure of the private traumas of Monroe and Ashe arguably contributed to the nightmares of their last days.[59] As the phrase goes, their stories had long since become "public property."

In the film industry stardom adds its own twists because the actor/star has one foot in two worlds: in the frozen narratives of completed films as well as the shifting circumstances of their own public lives. As they navigate the uncertain paths of their ongoing lives they cannot help but provide new "revelations" that can change our attitudes toward them. Such was the fate of Joan Crawford, Ingrid Bergman, O. J. Simpson, and many others. Stardom destabilizes our understanding of a character. In *All About Eve* or *Celebrity* we are primed to ask if we watching a facile "performance," or the inner self revealed in the context of a role. Where does "the method" end and the "authentic" self begin? In one form or another, these kinds of questions have long been asked of performers known for their reliable recreations of a core persona. As with the 2001 film *The Anniversary Party*, where celebrity actors *are playing* celebrity actors in the midst of various career crises, the characters already seem to be in their own skins.

This merging of private and public has not destroyed the possibility of creating enduring identifications, but it has probably skewed them away from the "cathartic" or "allegiance-producing" forms described at the beginning of this chapter. The reasons seem to lie in the fact that celebrity in all of its forms seems to be a cyclical process that takes as well as gives. In an age that thrives on irony and the will to never be "taken in," positive and potent allegiance-producing identifications seem to invite the destructive virus of unmasking. With many exceptions, the "down" phase of this cycle often destroys idealizations that the "up" phase has created. Sympathetic personas initially constructed around "front-region" actions are often undone as the cycle completes itself with "revelations" and "inconsistencies" that surface in back-region behaviors. The presence of the new and sometimes dissonant information deprives us of sentimental identifications: preferred associations that cannot be rewritten by the next day's headlines. It easy to see why fans of the Victorian novel or the films of Frank Capra want to return to their familiar and safe worlds.

What is attainable in an age that demystifies celebrity are levels of identification that seem similar to what Smith labeled "recognition" and P. David Marshall called "sympathetic identification." At these levels sympathy and empathy flow from the universals of human experience rather than judgments of moral superiority. They allow us to place ourselves in the position of a suffering and imperfect figure, even if they fall short of enacting our own values.

Of course Marshall and Smith were describing the possibilities for figures from film and fiction. It's important to remember the promise of fictional narrative generally is that its characters have the means to escape the downside of the celebrity cycle even if public figures cannot. The agents that move the plot along live safely on celluloid or between the covers of a novel. The times may change, but their essential nature does not. It is not surprising that many of the estates of writers are reluctant to license "updates" or permit commercial use of their of original personages.[60] Tom Sawyer, Scarlett O'Hara, and Atticus Finch are national treasures in their original incarnations. Their essential natures are fixed, and our identification with them is likely to remain stable.

Lessons from the Age of Celebrity

Film has enriched our understanding of the levels of intensity created in the process of living through another character. In the parallel worlds of politics, sports, and other spheres of public life, emulation works in similar ways. Based on the ways various players on the national stage are portrayed, we form attitudes, establish passions, and—through the unfolding details of *their* lives—acknowledge and affirm our *own* relationship to the society.[61]

As I have argued here, we are increasingly part of a culture that deflects interest in public *acts* and partly redirects it to the consideration of personal *attributes*. Such is the nature of stardom and celebrity, as well as our obsession with the personal over the public self. The drama of our national life is now seen as much from the wings as from the "front of the house." This side view perspective has the effect of making us an insider to someone else's performance.[62] We see the actor in the process of creating the role, and we are fascinated by the transformation from their public to their private selves.

Because we see others in multiple and sometimes contradictory roles, single and durable identifications are less likely. An array of disclosed attributes from the private realm can alienate as well as endear: a process that has important consequences for figures beyond the entertainment world. When Nell Painter began work on a biography of Sojourner Truth, she recalls, "I thought if I were sitting here and Sojourner Truth came and sat down, we could have a comfortable conversation." But intimate knowledge of the famous slave preacher actually put more distance between the author and her subject. As Painter learned more about her and "more about the period, her closeness to me receded and she became less and less and less familiar. And so now I think if she were sitting here, I would just have to listen."[63]

Identification thrives on first impressions and limited knowledge. It withers in the glare of sustained attention and historical revisionism. One wonders if Franklin Roosevelt could have ever launched his successful 1932 bid for the presidency if there had been widespread public knowledge of his unconventional and estranged relationship with Eleanor.[64] Similarly, would knowledge of John Kennedy's crippling Addison's disease and extramarital affairs have ruined his prospects in 1960?[65] There may have been a time when any chance to question the president was, in Max Frankel's words, "an act of high purpose."[66] But we now exist in an era where all journalism tends to feed on revelations of the personal represented as potential violations of public norms. Perhaps this is why we have so many more celebrities than true heroes. Where the informational domain of the hero is stable, celebrity is far more transient. While film characters give us permanent and self-contained representations, stars represent unfinished narratives with unpredictable outcomes. Even our relationships with the deceased have become unstable. They are now subject to the biographer's autopsy, motivated by the modern impulse to find the hidden pathologies they kept from us.

Chapter 4

SERENADES TO THE RESISTANT

Successful Uses of Identification

Hell, if I'd stayed in there much longer, he'd have had me coming out for civil rights.
—George Wallace, after meeting with Lyndon Johnson

Bill Clinton was strangely malleable, a creature of his audience, besotted with his ability to charm, constantly trying to please.

—Joe Klein, *The Natural*

The very core of our sociality resides not just in our consciousness of others, but in our capacity to partly inhabit the "place" of someone else. For example, we accept the fact that novelists and dramatists can construct plausible characters very different from themselves. The iconic figures of Harry Potter, Hercule Poirot, Tracy Lord, Atticus Finch, and Margo Channing are all creations of writers of the opposite sex. But they all seem to be authentic parts of the narrative universe invented by their authors. *The Philadelphia Story's* Tracy Lord was well cast with a young Katharine Hepburn. Yet the character of the independent-minded socialite was equally the product of playwright Philip Barry and director George Cukor. Cukor was regarded as an ideal director of women, having built a career working with a number of actresses to achieve career-defining roles.[1]

We may sometimes be surprised by the gap that exists between a story and the very different biography of its teller. Rhetors and artists can show a remarkable empathy for settings that are

71

alien to their own. Aaron Copland wrote what many regard as music that captures the essence of the American experience: the hymns and elegies of middle America in "Appalachian Spring," the plainsong to accompany the action of "Our Town" and "The Red Pony," and the evocative western motifs in the ballet scores for "Rodeo" and "Billy the Kid." And yet Copland was raised in Brooklyn, the son of Jewish Russian immigrants, trained in Paris, and not particularly secretive about his homosexuality.[2] The capacity for identification defies easy stereotypes.

Copland's assimilation into the American mainstream was also duplicated on a grander scale by the men who founded the Hollywood studios. Virtually every major studio was the product of enterprising Jewish families who had immigrated to the United States from Eastern Europe. But in spite of their status as recent immigrants, as Neal Gabler points out, they managed to give us quintessential images of American life.[3] These Russian and Polish Jews created venerable institutions that dramatized our most enduring myths about the virtues of small-town life, strong families, and earnest middle-class values. In films such as *On Moonlight Bay* (1951), *Life With Father* (1947), and *Meet Me in St. Louis* (1944), all of the pieties we wanted to believe about the essence of America were intact. *Moonlight Bay*, for example, offered a sunny romance between Marjorie Winfield (Doris Day) and William Sherman (Gordon McRae) in a mythic America common to Booth Tarkington's stories and Norman Rockwell's pictures. Yet those who invented Hollywood had deeper roots in New York's lower East side than in the perfect Indiana town that was the setting for Marjorie's transition from tomboy to a young woman. Ironically, even second-generation Hollywood moguls like Jack and Harry Warner, who produced *Moonlight Bay*, would have still been denied access to the country clubs of the WASPs who especially cherished these cinematic myths.[4]

The focus of this chapter and the next is on attempts to transcend one's own history to achieve effective persuasion. The very heart of identification lies in the opportunity—and it is always just an opportunity—to create a shared universe through words, actions, and images. Chapter 5 focuses on efforts that, for various reasons, fell short. The emphasis here is on messages that were ingeniously constructed to bridge significant differences. In their details we find the essential universals of identification: the resources of rhetoric that offer serenades to the resistant.

There is obviously an enormous universe of cases to choose from. One could try to account for the surprising success of Eve Ensler's meditation on one body part in *The Vagina Monologues*. Against considerable odds (at least to a male) it seems to have captured the desire of women around the world to celebrate and sometimes mourn the layers of attitudes associated with their own biology. Most theatrical works have audiences measured in the thousands. But even though Ensler's script is usually read by three women on an empty stage, it has attracted millions. There is also the unusual story of 90 inmates in a British psychiatric hospital who somehow connected with the paradoxes of Shakespeare's King Lear. Against the odds of their incarceration, notes actor Brian Cox, they loved the Shakespearean jokes, and understood better than most audiences the Fool's delight in undermining Lear's authority.[5]

A similar skill at closing the distance between audience and context is identified by Elizabeth Giddens, who notes the subtle forms of identification employed in John McPhee's widely admired sojourns into the natural world. His book on Alaska, *Coming Into the Country*, uses the persona of a nonexpert everyman to establish connections "between Alaskans, the author, and readers, making the experiences of the first two accessible to the latter."[6] McPhee's acceptance and tolerance of the pluralism that is built into his travels is itself a model for identification, notes Giddens, because pluralism is itself "a philosophy that requires identification."[7]

McPhee's work typically takes the strangeness out of a subject. It anticipates a pluralistic audience. The same pattern of bridging natural differences is common to politics, as can be seen in the remarkable identification of less affluent Americans with the wealthy Roosevelts of Hyde Park, New York. Franklin and Eleanor Roosevelt were unlikely populists, having been raised in the Hudson valley to carry on the blueblood traditions of their respective families. But they grew beyond their aristocratic and sometimes unhappy childhoods, growing into leaders who commanded deep loyalty. Lower-income voters, union members, and immigrants rarely wavered in their identification with the couple.[8]

The two cases examined in this chapter come from this realm of national politics and the presidency. Presidential rhetoric has the advantage of transparency; its appeals are inclusive and earnest. We focus on two moments when a chief executive managed to effectively patch together a message of unity in the face of considerable opposition. The cases are additionally interesting because each represents a president at war with the limitations of his own biography. Lyndon Johnson's voting rights speech of 1965 abandoned the states rights traditions honored by his southern colleagues. Its effect was to dramatically move the nation's civil rights agenda forward, and it remains as a monument to the possibilities of presidential leadership. Bill Clinton's 1993 address at the Vietnam Veteran's Memorial offers a more modest lesson. His speech was never intended to be more than it was: a ceremonial gesture. But in its own way it illustrates the effective use of the available tropes of the office: appeals to familiar values that are all the most interesting because of his low credibility with the American military.

In both messages we see interesting applications of the principle of identification, creating unity where others—especially the press—tended to see only division. Both speeches presumed a polity defined by its common experiences. And in compelling ways, each message partly succeeds in making those presumptions binding on their audiences.

Outflanking His Friends: Johnson's Enactment of the Voting Rights Act

In the 1960s few Americans would have predicted that one of the most important advances in racial justice would be engineered by a southern politician whose first vote in Congress was against an antilynching law. Lyndon Johnson was an unlikely prospect as the leader who would find the will to end American political apartheid.[9] Most Americans had believed that John Kennedy would be the civil rights president of the modern era.[10] But for reasons that go beyond his premature death—among them, a penchant for political caution hidden in the rhetoric of progressive change—it was not to be.

Johnson's rise to national prominence in the United States Senate had been helped enormously by Richard Russell, a titan in the annals of deliberative politics, a masterful tactician, and an unrepentant racist. Johnson looked to the older man for help in learning the folkways and customs of the Senate. And Johnson's small-town origins matched Russell's interest in federal action to ease the effects of poverty. Russell also understood the Senate's rules and traditions better than anyone, cobbling together bipartisan compromises to enact the passage of key pieces of New Deal legislation.[11] But even though he was a more sophisticated legislator than most of his Southern colleagues, Russell shared their deep suspicion of black Americans. Along with a handful of governors from the region, he represented a formidable roadblock to meaningful civil rights legislation.[12]

Then as now, American political culture reflected the values of the south far more than any other part of the nation. Southern members in safe seats usually remained in office longer and gained greater seniority. And so Johnson and later heirs to leadership positions learned to acquire the Senate's distinctly southern traditions: the outward courtesy of its members, its more leisurely pace, and its sense of distance from the crush of public opinion. But in his rise to Senate majority leader, and eventually the presidency, he lost his taste for another Southern custom: an interest in perpetuating the politics of race veiled in the language of states rights.[13]

As unlikely as it now seems, as late as 1965 the principle of "one person one vote" was still a novel and dangerous idea to Russell from Georgia, James Eastland of Mississippi, South Carolina's Strom Thurmond, Governor George Wallace of Alabama, and many others. But its time had clearly come. And with Johnson's hand forced by Alabama police violence against Martin Luther King's Selma marchers, he would have to act sooner rather than later. A full one hundred years after the Civil War, Johnson finally closed the legal loopholes that kept the rolls of registered black voters in Alabama, Mississippi, and other states to a tiny fraction of truly eligible voters. And he did so by neutralizing opposition in a very public address that denied honor to anyone trying to defeat the legislation.

Johnson's speech to a joint session of Congress on the evening of March 15 leveraged the Congress to act. The resulting bill would have a profound effect on the political landscape, making it possible for blacks to enter into the political life of the south. Prior to the enactment of the Voting Rights Act of 1965, there were only a few hundred African American officeholders in the United States. By 1990 the number had risen to 6000.[14] And within a few years of its passage, most of the Southern states had moved from 6 or 7 percent voter registration to around 50 percent: the minimum set by the act if a state wanted to avoid the presence of federal voter registrars.[15] Rarely had a piece of federal legislation so rapidly and completely altered the balance of power in one region of the nation.

Martin Luther King's planned march from Selma to Montgomery—along with the overreactions of George Wallace's Alabama—gave the president the forward momentum he needed to trump discriminatory voter registration practices. King's goal had been to engage in a march of about 50 miles. He was enough of a seasoned activist to know that he was offering the kind of bait to Alabama's racist police that they might find hard to resist. In turn, television and newspaper images of the violence against the march would further pull at the conscience of the nation. What King could not of know at the time is that the march would create a photographic benchmark in the struggle for civil rights: a moment that would fix in time the senseless brutality of a discredited and dying order. In his memoirs Johnson recalled the horrors that most Americans had seen on the evening news:[16]

> The singing came to an abrupt end early in the evening of March 7, when the marchers reached the Edmund Pettus Bridge at the southern edge of Selma and were confronted by Sheriff Jim Clark and a mounted posse. The sheriff ordered the marchers to turn around. They knew their rights and refused. The Alabama state troopers took matters into their own hands. With nightsticks, bullwhips, and billy clubs, the scattered the ranks of the marchers. More than fifty men and women were severely injured. The march was over.[17]

Along with an increasing majority of Americans, Johnson sensed a newer level of racial hatred that threatened to metastasize into a national disaster. In several days it would fall to him to call the widow of a white Unitarian minister who had just been killed in Selma, beaten by whites as a "nigger lover." "I had no answer to the one question that kept turning over in my mind" he noted. "How many . . . will die before our country is truly free?"[18]

Johnson's decision to follow-up after Selma with a prime-time speech to a joint session of the Congress was a dramatic move, and the highwater mark of his presidency. It had been nineteen years since a president had appeared before the combined body to ask for passage of legislation.[19] And this event gained even more importance because of the huge audiences who would see it on television. On this night he mastered the primary instrument for the orchestration of American public opinion: the same instrument that would defeat him in just three short years. In that time his coalition-building talents would be undone by television news footage of a bloody Vietnam, and he would decline to run for a second term. But all of that was still in the future. Television news footage of Selma had the reverse effect of priming the American public to accept his message. It made racism embarrassingly visible and ugly.

Arguably, no president since Lincoln had ever committed himself as completely and magnificently to the cause of civil rights and economic enfranchisement. As Robert Dallek noted, the speech "elevated himself and his presidency to a higher plane."[20]

Johnson began by placing events in Selma in the ongoing saga of "man's unending search for freedom. So it was at Lexington and Concord. So it was a century ago at Appomatox. So it was last week in Selma, Alabama."[21] His words were measured and his stare was penetrating. Anyone who had ever made the mistake of resisting his appeals knew the unmistakable signs: Johnson was confident he would prevail. Like a seaman with the winds at his back and few obstacles ahead, he acted as if nothing would change him from his course.

> Rarely in any time does an issue lay bare the secret heart of America itself. Rarely are we met with a challenge, not to our growth or abundance, or our welfare or our security, but rather to the values and purposes and the meaning of our beloved nation. The issue of equal rights for American Negroes is such an issue.... There is no Negro problem. There is no Southern problem. There is no Northern problem. There is only an American problem.[22]

He was just finishing the first minutes of a speech that would run nearly an hour in length and would be interrupted 36 times by applause. But it was quickly becoming apparent that he intended to put his considerable credibility on the line for this bill. Invoking statements from the canon of American beliefs—"All men are created Equal," "Give me Liberty or give me Death,"—he would add freedom to vote as a right that "Americans fought and died for."[23]

Protectors of the old south sat in immobile silence as he turned what some thought might be a simple message for a racial truce into an insistent demand for legislative action. Before the evening was over, he reminded the packed chamber of his own early years as a school teacher to poor white and Hispanic kids, noting that he never dreamt then "that I might have the chance to help the sons and daughters of those students. . . . But now I do have that chance. And I'll let you in on a secret—I mean to use it."

There are moments in every presidency when it becomes clear that events have been defined as a provocation. Leaders must choose these moments carefully because they know that if they define an event as a national crisis, they must prevail. Johnson's confidence as a senate deal-maker no doubt contributed to his decision to draw a line in the sand: to announce that what had long prevailed must now end.

The problem, of course, was abundantly clear. Local voter registrars used a variety of tests and taxes to turn back African American citizens who tried to register:

> There is no reason which can excuse the denial of that right. There is no duty which weighs more heavily on us than the duty we have to insure that right. Yet the harsh fact is that in many places in this country men and women are kept from voting simply because they are Negroes. Every device of which human ingenuity is capable has been used to deny this right. The Negro citizen may go to register only to be told that the day is wrong, or the hour is late, or the official in charge is absent. And if he persists and, if he manages to present himself to the registrar, he may be disqualified because he did not spell out his middle name, or because he abbreviated a word on the application. And if he manages to fill out an application, he is given a test.
>
> The registrar is the sole judge of whether he passes this test. He may be asked to recite the entire Constitution, or explain the most complex provisions of state law.
>
> And even a college degree cannot be used to prove that he can read or write. For the fact is that the only way to pass these barriers is to show a white skin.[24]

Johnson went on to note that within a few days the Congress would receive a voting rights bill that would give the federal government the power to register voters in states where minority voter registration remained below 50 percent. Southern voter registrars who flouted the rules would find officials of the United States government in their districts taking over their duties. "Open your polling places to all your people," he urged. "Allow men and women to register to vote whatever their color of their skin."

The President was never one to rush through a message. But at this point he paused for extra effect, and then began again slowly:

> There is no constitutional issue here. The command of the Constitution is plain. There is no moral issue. It is wrong— deadly wrong—to deny any of your fellow Americans the right to vote in this country.

A tide of applause rose from the crowd, and Johnson waited to move on with a characteristic half-smile of satisfied determination: "There is no issue of state's rights or national rights. There is only the struggle for human rights."[25]

One can only guess what traditional opponents to civil rights measures must have thought this late in the speech. But it was increasingly clear that *this* message from *this* source was quickly turning the evening into their worst nightmare. Surely he will stop, they must have hoped. Surely he was finished with his careless identification of the presidency with the rag-tag groups of demonstrators and marchers who had forced themselves into the headlines. Didn't he know that they had provoked southern leaders? Where was his anger for the intemperate rhetoric of civil rights leaders who had made them out to be custodians of a separatist gulag?

But Johnson had barely reached the midpoint of his address. The speech would tie up the networks for most of prime time, carrying the heft and length of a State of the Union address. In the remaining twenty minutes he took his and future presidencies irrevocably into a role of activism for racial equality:

> This time, on this issue, there must be no delay, or no hesitation, or no compromise with our purpose. We cannot, we must not, refuse to protect the right of every American to vote in every election that he may desire to participate in. . . . We have already waited 100 years and more and the time for waiting is gone.[26]

Few could have anticipated what would happen next. At some point it became clear that the speech was not just another routine journey through a litany of "concerns." His commitment was so deep, his identification with the legislation so total, that to defeat it would risk too much. He had invoked the "outraged conscience of a nation" to press for a new piece of civil rights legislation. But now his language was about to shift in a stunning direction:

> What happened in Selma is part of a larger movement which reaches into every section and state of America. It is the effort of American Negroes to secure for themselves the full blessings of American life. Their cause must be our cause too. Because it's not just Negroes, but really it's all of us, who must overcome the crippling legacy of bigotry and injustice.

Johnson then paused for emphasis.

And we shall overcome.

It was an electric moment. A president who declared that his "roots go deeply into Southern soil" had dared to utter the lines of *The Movement*. He had accepted and used the poetry of the cause. It was the language despised by Southern obstructionists, some of them sitting before him. And before the evening was over he would use the phrase once more as a reminder that it had not been a coincidence. Few were prepared for this chief executive to invest the movement with this signifier of legitimacy.

Richard Goodwin had worked with the president on the speech and was standing in the well of the House at that moment. He saw tears in the faces of hardened legislators, many of whom thought they would never hear such an unequivocal expression of solidarity with black America. The moment is vividly captured in his memoirs:

> There was an instant of silence, the gradually apprehended realization that the president had proclaimed, adopted as his own rallying cry, the anthem of black protest, the hymn of a hundred embattled black marches. Seventy-seven-year-old Congressman Manny Celler—a lifetime of vigorous, often futile fights for freedom behind him—leaped to his feet, cheering as wildly as a schoolboy at his first football game.

Others quickly followed. In seconds almost the entire chamber—floor and gallery together—was standing; applauding, shouting, some stamping their feet. Tears rolled down the cheeks of Senator Mansfield of Montana. Senator Ellender of Louisiana slumped in his seat. In distant Alabama, Martin Luther King cried; while groups around thousands of television sets in university halls and private homes, millions of people, especially the young, felt a closeness—an almost personal union—with their government. . . . I felt it too—the urge toward tears which was not the edge of grief or of some simple leisure, but some more profoundly human need to be a part of something greater and more noble than oneself.

God, how I loved Lyndon Johnson at that moment.[27]

On this day the Congress had become a great stage set, and—and least for some—the president for some had become a cathartic hero: the master and embodiment of moral action. There would be no balancing phrases about the excesses of the civil rights movement, no criticism of the tactics of Martin Luther King or anyone else, no softening of tone for the sake of his congressional friends who would oppose the legislation. Johnson only cautioned against seeing the problem of full integration in purely in Southern terms. "There is really no part of America," he noted, "where the promise of equality has been fully kept."

And he gave credit where it was largely due. Johnson was not an admirer of King. And in the days before Selma, the White House was regularly picketed by civil rights activists, some of whom had managed to penetrate the building for vocal and short-lived sit ins.[28] But he resisted the strong political inclination to find scapegoats:

The real hero of this struggle is the American Negro. His actions and protests, his courage to risk safety, and even to risk his life, have awakened the conscience of this nation. His demonstrations have been designed to call attention to injustice, designed to provoke change; designed to stir reform. He has called upon us to make good the promise of America. And who among us can say that we would have made the same progress were it not for his persistent bravery and his faith in American democracy?[29]

If anyone needed further evidence of Johnson's commitment to the issue, he closed by offering his own experience as a coda. He referred to his teaching days in Cotulla, Texas. Even as a novice educator in the small Mexican-American school, he could see the corrosive effects of poverty and discrimination. The description showed a characteristic melancholy that he usually kept out of public view:

> My students were poor and they often came to class without breakfast and hungry. And they knew even in their youth the pain of prejudice. They never seemed to know why people disliked them, but they knew it was so because I saw it in their eyes. . . . And somehow you never forget what poverty and hatred can do when you see its scars on the hopeful face of a young child.[30]

And so he came to his observation that in 1928 he never dreamt he would have the chance to help the sons and daughters of his students. His conclusion that it was not an opportunity he could pass up brought the crowded chamber to its feet yet again in a standing ovation.

With this speech governmental activism on civil rights had a greater presumption of legitimacy. Four years earlier President John Kennedy and Attorney General Robert Kennedy often sought to moderate between Southern politicos and civil rights leaders, using private backchannels and publicly urging forbearance.[31] Johnson's approach was a marked contrast. He invoked a string of potent American first principles that dealt piecemeal incrementalism a significant blow. Their force dramatically raised the price of opposition to the movement. This bill and an earlier one in 1964 was now *his cause* and—through the instrumentality of the speech—*the nation's cause.* Civil rights workers were now the sanctioned agents of essential change; and resistance to equal participation in the electoral process deserved the backlash of indignation that Selma had spawned. To now work to defeat or amend the bill would come at the high price of appearing to be on the margins of America, to be part of its darker past.

After lopsided votes in favor of the bill in both houses, Johnson signed the act into law six months later. Throughout the southern states, blacks were enfranchised in large numbers for the first time. But equally significant, it was now far less acceptable to use racist appeals to win election or hold public office. Making African Americans the *constituents* of officeholders was far more empowering than many had envisioned. Racist appeals now had diminishing returns for elected officials, who would have to deliver services and embrace inclusion, or else pay the price at the polls.

Searching for a Common Past: Bill Clinton at the Vietnam Memorial

In the same month Lyndon Johnson asked Congress to reconcile America's values with its promises, the freshman-class president at a university a few miles from the capitol met with other student leaders to decide if funds should be used to support civil rights marches in Selma and elsewhere. The nineteen-year-old Bill Clinton thought Georgetown students should participate in the marches, though he was less certain it was reasonable to use student money.[32] America's dismal record on civil rights and its increasing commitment to the Vietnam War consumed Clinton as he progressed through Georgetown, and then on to an additional two years at Oxford as a Rhodes Scholar.

The chance to go to England on the prestigious scholarship was an early sign of his famously outsized capacity to absorb the world around him. But in many other ways Clinton was like many other "boomers" in this period. Rising levels of affluence bankrolled the emergence of a separate youth culture that celebrated opposition to the aging conventions of the mainstream. Larger numbers of students had the luxury of more time and income than the prior World War II generation. And while many used their financial freedom to subsidize a junior version of their parent's lifestyle, the more civic conscious were also aware of the social effects of American prosperity. In the familiar idiom of those moving through its universities, America had become fat and complacent: too ready to believe its myths of moral superiority, and too accepting of the injustices that contradicted its stated ideals. For the first time in over a hundred years, war had ceased to be a touchstone of common national pride. It would soon divide the young intelligencia from the mainstream in ways that would open deep and lasting wounds.[33]

In his civil rights activism and his antiwar efforts Clinton fit in to this new mold. He memorized speeches by Martin Luther King, and chided his friends for their ambivalence toward American militarism.[34] An internship with J. William Fulbright and the Senate Foreign Relations Committee placed him in the one congressional setting where doubts about the wisdom of the war could flourish. Fulbright was the leading congressional critic of the Johnson administration's expansion of American involvement in the war, and all the more persuasive for his thoughtful and patient manner. Clinton seemed to emulate the senator's style of respectful dissent, never seriously abandoning establishment politics for the more adversarial style of the antiwar New Left.[35]

Even so, it would be hard to underestimate the dread that hung over him as he pondered the prospect of being drafted into military service in Vietnam. To the University of Arkansas ROTC director who had helped Clinton get one deferment, he wrote that his job with the committee allowed him to work "against a war opposed and despised with a depth of feeling I had reserved solely for racism in America."[36] In Washington and while at Oxford he took part in several protests, befriended a number of activists, grew a beard, and tried to explain his opposition to his friends and himself. He was also fascinated with the stormy events in the Soviet bloc, and—like many of his classmates—traveled on both sides of Europe's East/West divide. He was acutely aware of his own moral quandary. By 1969, 39 thousand men had already died in Vietnam. And most of the several million drafted by the Selective Service reluctantly put their lives on hold and turned themselves over to the military, even though many had little enthusiasm for the war.

One looks in vain through the histories of other modern presidents to find a similar crisis of confidence about the actions of the government.[37] But Clinton came of age at the moment of the nation's deepest crisis since the Civil War. A series of national traumas undermined public faith in the virtues of American life: the continuing Vietnam quagmire, the assassinations of Martin Luther King and Robert Kennedy, and a growing discomfort among the socially aware over the gap between America's poor and its wealthy. Circumstance and inclination had placed Clinton in the position of becoming the first heir to the modern presidency to have taken tentative steps away from the presumptive center of American politics.

In the 1992 political campaign George Bush and other Republican surrogates saw an opening, and chipped away at Clinton's youthful choices. Partly because his college at Oxford had sought to protect two Czechoslovakian students after the Soviets had cracked down on dissidents, Clinton made an effort to visit one of their parents in Prague at the end of his trip across the continent.[38] The nativist mentality of some Americans made it possible to connect the dots in such a way that this all added up to something close to treason. Without having to take full responsibility for the assertion, George Bush senior suggested as much in a campaign interview with CNN's Larry King:

> I don't want to tell you what I really think because I don't have the facts. But to go to Moscow one year after Russia crushed Czechoslovakia, not to remember what you saw? . . . You can remember who you saw in the airport in Oslo, but you can't remember who you saw in the airport in Moscow? I say level with the American people on the draft, whether you went to Moscow, how many demonstrations he led against his country from foreign soil.[39]

In the context of the campaign, these attacks turned out to be a serious miscalculation. It was hardly unusual that thousands of American students flocked to Europe every year, and that many wanted to see the Soviet Union and its satellites. Americans also understood that there was now a whole new generation of office seekers with no military past, including a rising Republican star named Newt Gingrich.[40] Bush's innuendoes were understood by many for what they were: a diversion by an incumbent who seemed reluctant to spend much time talking about his own presidency.

But in spite of public suspicions over the motives of the Bush campaign, efforts to make Clinton's past *the* issue of 1992 entered the field of public discussion and never quite left. A persona that combined sex, drugs, and political activism somehow matched the times, which now converted presidential campaigns into another aspect of celebrity culture. He would have to deal with that legacy in the first tentative days of his new administration.

In one of his first acts as President, Clinton took a fateful step that would highlight the paradox of a commander in chief who had no prior military experience. He affirmed a campaign promise to end discrimination against gays in all branches of the military. Clinton had raised the issue several times in the campaign without garnering much publicity or opposition. He had long thought the military's expensive efforts to entrap and prosecute homosexuals were counterproductive. In one year alone, the military had spent 22 million dollars to discharge and replace gay men and women, who were liable for prosecution for a felony crime under the Uniform Code of Military Justice.[41] Ignoring the deeply ingrained military culture that cherished conventional views of masculinity, he argued that individuals in the services "should be judged based on their behavior, not their lifestyle."[42] Within the White House there seemed to be a naïve hope that a quick executive order could be done without another battle in the nation's ongoing culture wars. But that was a severe blunder.

Clinton's decision to end the ban became an ongoing news story, fed by statements of opposition by the military's conservative friends on Capitol Hill, and by military leaders themselves. Over months of protracted meetings the Joint Chiefs of Staff dug in their heels, making it more difficult to find a solution the administration could sell to them and to an uneasy public. As communications director George Stephanopoulos noted, the story began to spin out of control:

> We scrambled to quiet the political storm. . . . But we soon found ourselves trapped between the military brass who wanted no change, gay leaders who insisted on all or nothing, delighted Republicans who couldn't wait to vote against us, and appalled Democrats who couldn't believe that gays in the military was going to be their first vote with a new president.[43]

The real cost, of course, was that the issue affirmed Clinton's status as an outsider on military affairs. The opposition of the highly regarded Colin Powell especially hurt. The decorated African American head of the Joint Chiefs of Staff was fluent, thoughtful, and effective with the media. He was a hero of the Persian Gulf War and hardly the person to be tagged as an intolerant bigot. And the resulting clash of personalities and cultures made the perfect news story. Since the expulsion of gays did not provoke the same anger in the American public as earlier civil rights cases that focused on race or religion, it was easier for the press to frame the story as a political miscalculation rather than a fight against discrimination. Here was a commander in chief, they noted, who was imposing alien values on the armed services even while he was being instructed in the proper way to give a military salute.

It was against these events that Bill Clinton approached the first major military holiday in his new presidency. It would be his job to preside over a number of Memorial Day events, including a speech a few days before to graduating cadets at West Point and the laying of the traditional wreath at Arlington National Cemetery. But the key event of the weekend would be a brief address at the Vietnam Veterans Memorial.

The long wedge of black granite carved into the soil on the wide side of the mall is the most visited shrine in the capitol, and the one that brings up all the contradictory emotions veterans and older Americans still associate with the war. Visitors are unusually quiet at this site, pausing to touch the indentations of one of the 58,000 names engraved into its long sloping face. Many who are now middle aged search for the specific name of a relative or school friend. Others move slowly along the infinity of small print, absorbing yet again the scale of the war's human cost.

The wall is a cemetery in all but name. It honors soldiers, and it officially observes a troubling moment in the nation's past. For some, it also provides a gravestone for America's cherished faith in military invincibility, and for others it represents a nation without the courage to live up to its political hubris. Tourists use many of the older monuments as playgrounds. But at this place feelings of anger, shame, or despair are never very far below the surface.

The decision to appear at the war shrine came as a surprise to many. No previous president had ever accepted an invitation to give a Memorial Day address at the site. And many hoped Clinton would decline. A letter from a veteran to the *Houston Chronicle* caught the tone of a postcard campaign asking him not to come:

Many of the names on the wall of the Vietnam Memorial belong to servicemen who died because of the politics of antiwar activism. The children of privilege from America's elite universities, like Clinton, have a lot to answer for. They did not serve their country, often for selfish rather than idealistic reasons, and adopted fashionable antiwar attitudes that eroded public support for the war. . . .[44]

The president's eight-minute address was preceded by remarks from Colonial Janis Nark, a nurse, who told of her initial reluctance to visit the wall. Secretary of Veterans Affairs Jesse Brown and Colin Powell also spoke, both offering comments intended to shield Clinton from a crowd of about a thousand protesters kept well behind the invited guests in the front seats. Brown made note of Clinton's support for jobless and homeless veterans.[45] And Powell, then the most senior military official in the nation, invoked Lincoln's Second Inaugural—"with malice towards none, with charity for all"—to emphasize the need "to bind up the nation's wounds." In the few minutes of his introduction he used that phrase four times in the vain hope that it would subdue the rising din of taunts.

Where the audience a few days earlier at West Point had been deferential and supportive, many in this crowd were defiant and angry. Some came not to hear the president, but to protest his presence. The wall was *their* symbol, and Bill Clinton violated its sanctity. People standing behind the VIP seats shouted "coward," and "shame." And a scattering of hand-lettered signs carried the same bitter messages. The word "hypocrite" was scrawled across one. Another dripped with the vitriol that now passes for public discussion in our society: "Dodge the Draft, Smoke Dope, Cheat on Your Wife, Become President—the American Dream."[46]

Clinton began by thanking Powell and other earlier speakers for their remarks. But the jeers and boos continued: not enough to keep him from being heard, but enough to make an observer embarrassed at the spectacle. Modern presidents may be picketed or asked thorny questions. All the same, we have come to expect that others will honor him or at least his office with a civil hearing. For most public figures—even ones seasoned in the battles of a presidential campaign—this would have been a difficult challenge. But as scattered jeers continued, Clinton leaned into the microphone, took aim on the rowdy hecklers, and began a fascinating speech of accommodation.

"To all of you who are shouting, I have heard you. I ask you now to hear me. I have heard you." And they started to listen:

Some have suggested that it is wrong for me to be here with you today because I did not agree a quarter of a century ago with the decision made to send the young men and women to battle in Vietnam. Well, so much the better. Here we are celebrating America today. Just as war is freedom's cost, disagreement is freedom's privilege. And we honor it today.

But I ask all of you to remember the words that have been said here today, and I ask you, at this monument, can any American be out of place? And can any Commander in Chief be in any other place but here on this day? I think not.[47]

In an important rhetorical sense Clinton belongs with Theodore Roosevelt, F. D. R., and Lyndon Johnson. All four presidents thought there was no audience that they could not win over. All were ceaseless strivers, convinced that they could talk their way through any impasse. It was T. R. who identified the presidency as the "bully pulpit." And while F. D. R. came to lament his lack of control over the federal bureaucracy, he was supremely confident in the power of his personality.[48] As for Johnson, in the presence of others he simply refused to consider the possibility that someone could fail to yield to the commander-in-chief.[49]

Clinton's faith in the rhetorical inevitability of his appeals seemed to grow out of his fluency,[50] his considerable empathy for others, and the power of common ideas. Unlike Richard Nixon and both of the Bushes, he enjoyed the circus of political campaigns: events that could produce the same combative atmosphere as this speech. He acted like there was no disenfranchised constituency who could not be given refuge under the umbrella of his ideas. He gave the impression to people from vastly different social and economic strata that he found them interesting, and that he understood the passions that engaged them.

And so Clinton went to work, putting together a string of enthymetic conclusions that could by affirmed but not denied. The audience would be offered a script matching the formulaic requirements of the presidency. Commonplaces of the nation's shared history and values would be invoked, along with a tribute to the dead and to their children. He would also close with a pledge to make a complete governmental accounting of those still missing: the ultimate status issue for veterans convinced of a sinister conspiracy to foil the repatriation of their comrades.

His theme was simple. "Let us continue to disagree if we must about the war, but let us not let it divide us as a people any longer":

> Many volumes have been written about this war and those complicated times, but the message of this memorial is quite simple: These men and women fought for freedom, brought honor to their communities, loved their country and died for it. They were known to all of us. There's not a person in this crowd today who did not know someone on this wall. Four of my high school classmates are there, four who shared with me the joys and trials of childhood and did not live to see the three score and 10 years the Scripture says we are entitled to.[51]

These words smoothly placed Clinton himself in the context of the war and its heavy costs. To mock his thoughts now would also mock the memory of four soldiers from Hot Springs, Arkansas:

> No one has come here today to disagree about the heroism of those whom we honor. But the only way we can really honor their memory is to resolve to live and serve today and tomorrow as best we can and to make America the best that she can be. Surely that is what we owe to all those whose names are etched in this beautiful memorial.[52]

In three sentences the inclusive pronoun "we" is used four times. There is no dissenter's "I." The text is about common duties and responsibilities. We "honor" and we "owe":

> As we resolve to keep the finest military in the world, let us remember some of the lessons that all agree on. If the day should come when our service men and women must again go into combat, let us all resolve they will go with the training, the equipment, the support necessary to win, and most important of all, with a clear mission to win.

Clinton finds a way to embrace what many Vietnam veterans—including Colin Powell—came to believe about the war: that it reflected "a policy that had become bankrupt."[53] To be sure, there was no easy way to finesse the view that Clinton and other dissenters had weakened the nation's resolve to win. But the speech played to Clinton's greatest strength as president: his ability to connect with ordinary people. The commonplaces might be ordinary, but they resonate in the context of his apparent empathy.

> Let us do what is necessary to regain control over our destiny as a people here at home, to strengthen our economy and to develop the capacities of all of our people, to rebuild our communities and our families where children are raised and character is developed. Let us keep the American dream alive.

The totality of these comments represented about five minutes of this short address. The last closing moments were used to exploit his prerogatives as president to further the political objectives of the veteran's movement. The veterans still fighting at least the effects of the war would not go away empty-handed. Clinton promised to "renew a pledge to the families whose names are not on this wall because their sons and daughters did not come home." In an appeal that made more sense as a gesture of solidarity than an initiative that would produce tangible results, he noted that he would order the declassification of more government records regarding prisoners of war and those still missing in action. In 1993 there was only circumstantial evidence to support the view that North Vietnam was still holding back information on the location of the remains of American soldiers.[54] And just a year earlier the Senate held hearings that concluded that there was no credible evidence that Vietnam was holding living MIAs. But doubts about whether there was much more to learn from Hanoi were routinely dismissed by many of the five thousand or so activists who kept the POW/MIA issue alive. Throughout the 1990s they continued to view official Washington as complicit in an MIA cover-up.[55] The offer to pursue all avenues for additional information by declassifying over 1.5 million government documents[56] was thus a gift to the cause:

> As we allow the American public to have access to what our Government knows, we will press harder to find out what other governments know. We are pressing the Vietnamese to provide this accounting not only because it is the central outstanding issues in our relationship with Vietnam, but because it is a central commitment made by the American Government to our people. And I intend to keep it.[57]

Enthusiastic applause affirmed the fantasy that a chapter of military history still remained to be written. In a presidency defined by its ironies, critics could add another example. The previous president— a former navy pilot who had barely survived the crash of his own plane at sea—had declined to do what Clinton promised. But this was a leader who was forever tuning to find the dominant frequency of his audience. The pledge to open more files on MIAs delivered a measure of comfort.

Then to his close: a mixture of presidential vernacular merged with the recurring motif of Lincoln's Civil War call for "charity" in the place of "malice":

> Lincoln speaks to us today across the years. Let us resolve to take from this haunting and beautiful memorial a renewed sense of our national unity and purpose, a deepened gratitude for the sacrifice of those whose names we touched and whose memories we revere and a finer dedication to making America a better place for their children and for our children, too.
>
> Thank you all for coming here today, God bless you, and God bless America.[58]

The speech clearly demonstrated Clinton's capacity to find transcendent commonplaces. Like Johnson, he invoked the Civil War as a setting for building unity out of division. And in ways Burke would have found perversely revealing, even a brutal and divisive conflict somehow emerged as an affirmation of transcendent American values.

To be sure, the risks associated with Clinton's appearance at the memorial were also less than they seemed. A CBS poll released the day before the address found that nearly 70 percent of all veterans and even a higher percentage of nonveterans thought his visit was appropriate.[59] He and most of the world knew that the protesters were a minority, and—if we were to believe the images from Hollywood and various press accounts—a group that included some deeply troubled members.

The Limits of Rhetorical Other-Direction

Lyndon Johnson's civil rights address had the advantage of linking the nation's past struggles with promises still to be honored.

A vote for the Civil Rights Bill was a member's chance to identify with values that expressed the nation's better nature. Equal rights, Johnson compellingly argued, was a national birthright borne in the American Revolution and tested in the Civil War.

Though he would have wanted it otherwise, Clinton's speech turned on more problematic ideological identifications: some that had been rendered stale by the cynical times, and others that could not fully distract audiences from his divisive persona. The memory of Clinton's teenage opposition to war obviously loomed large on that day, and no doubt limited the extent to which he could produce the kind of personal and cinematic allegiance common in film and fiction.

Indeed, that is an important lesson to take from political discourse. In politics, identification with a value or a cause can be easier to sustain than identification with a person. What "conscious alignment" there is perhaps occurs mostly at the "associative" level described in the previous chapter. At this stage the discourse removes barriers between advocate and audience. There is a sense of active participation in dealing with a common experience. But the shared associations fall short of producing full allegiance with the agent.

This limitation was evident in both presidencies, but especially Clinton's. Fewer presidents have had greater gifts for understanding and communicating a sense of the common good. Former White House adviser David Gergen noted that Clinton had the rhetorical equivalent of "perfect pitch—an uncanny ability to read the mood of his audience."[60] But few have also faced so many obstacles in the path of political leadership. In addition to being a polarizing rather than unifying figure, there was also his disinclination to match his inclusive rhetoric with inclusive coalition-building.

Clinton was also an outsider to many in official Washington. He was often described as a leader who failed to effectively use the city's back channels to find common ground with legislative, business, and media leaders. In the words of Gergen, the president mastered the "outside game" of politics.[61] The "inside game" of patient coalition-building and accommodation with opponents was less of a strength. By contrast, Lyndon Johnson excelled at the inside game. Even if his speeches rarely achieved the grace of his civil rights address, he was notoriously effective in strong-arming his political opponents in private.[62] While Clinton often found a way to identify with specific interest groups focused on an activist domestic agenda (i.e., reformers in health care, gun control, and civil rights) he was less effective in negotiating with others and creating a sense of ongoing loyalty. Key items on the Clinton agenda—the proposed change of policy towards gays in the military, the push for a national health-care policy—tended to founder when opponents and legislators encountered an indifferent White House that was reluctant to bargain. For example, the White House planned the 1993–94 initiative for national health care as a full-fledged campaign, designing a number of vivid and effective public events to dramatize the human costs of a system that let too many citizens fall through the cracks. The massive health care overhaul ultimately failed for many reasons,[63] but significant among them was the fact that the Clinton White House was simply not prepared to negotiate with the Republican leadership in Congress over the legislative details.[64]

This is all a reminder that rhetorical identification has its limits. In the representational arts and other expressive media (i.e., film) identification may be the entire game: the supreme reward that a message can offer its audience. But in the realm of national politics, it is sometimes just a means to something else. Identification makes political rhetoric overtly populist. It represents the broadest impulses in the community by treating ideas as universal, thereby providing audiences with reasons to believe that they are more than spectators to their own civil life. Johnson's civil right address succeeded in part for this reason. But populism can also mask rather than neutralize opposing political forces: a fact that Clinton would discover repeatedly over his two terms.

The potential for presidential identification has also been limited by the cynical times to which Clinton was heir. Even the early 1990s was a time when the norm of rhetorical inclusion seemed especially at odds with a more fragmented and distrustful society. While other political operatives came to power and maintained it by exploiting division—Newt Gingrich and Tom DeLay in the House come to mind—Clinton was more constrained in the ways he could return their fire. George W. Bush was spared some of this presumptive disbelief by the momentous terrorist attacks on New York and Washington in 2001. But the fixed necessity for identification through inclusive rhetorical other direction sometimes makes it seem as if the president is the last living "straight man" on the planet: the last person in the culture to try to reach people without a trace of doubt, cynicism, or sarcasm. He is an earnest person in an age of irony: the object of endless unmasking and debunking in a popular press that has all but abandoned the lines between political news and commentary.

The deeper problems of constructing an inclusive rhetoric in an age of fragmentation are explored more fully in the next two chapters, but it is enough to note here that the news media and the public are somewhat disinclined to take such rhetorics of obligation, honor, or sacrifice at face value. The idea that "things are not what they seem" used to be a literary convention. Now, it is a principle for judging any public rhetoric. Against appeals to obligation we see self-serving opportunity. Instead of accepting references to the honor and sacrifice of Vietnam's veterans, we see the paradox of Clinton's efforts to avoid military service. Attributions of motive have always loomed large in how we calculate a message. But we now accept the premise that the manifest motives of public figures are always suspect.

These forces require caution in claiming success for Clinton's message. In the end, this fascinating "serenade" to a restless audience probably changed few minds. For some it was a calculated moment with no compensating benefits. For others it seemed to represent an honorable attempt to reconcile old and deep differences, while fulfilling an important obligation of the office. Perhaps the judgment of an Army veteran from Wyoming caught this more upbeat mood best. "I may not agree with you," he remarked as he offered Clinton his hand, "but that took courage."[65]

Chapter 5

MISIDENTIFICATION AND ITS SOURCES

But alas, we are not of one heart or mind.
—Harold Barrett, *Rhetoric and Civility*

During his Presidential campaign, he delivered speeches in Memphis and Raleigh advocating the elimination of federal cotton subsidies; in Knoxville, he proposed selling the Tennessee Valley Authority's steam generating plants; in West Virginia, he denounced the war on poverty...
—Louis Menand, describing Barry Goldwater

In his furtive run for the White House in 1992, Texas industrialist Ross Perot created the rhetorical equivalent of a train wreck in what should have been a routine address at the national convention of the NAACP. Politicians seeking the presidency know that the venerable civil rights organization is an essential stop. It offers the chance—indeed, the requirement—to demonstrate at least a level of ideological solidarity with the African American community. Perhaps politicians better than industrialists sense the need to present themselves as kindred spirits. And that was clearly Perot's intent, signaled with references to his poor family, and the admiration in his hometown for its black churches and their values. Most of his standard stump speech about the unsteady economy drew cautious applause, but as he tried to align himself with the audience's concerns, the pronoun "you" kept getting in the way.

The simple word reappeared several times in the wrong places, not unlike an uninvited stranger at a family reunion. "Financially at least, it's going to be a long, hot summer," he told the conferees. "Now I don't have to tell you who gets hurt first when this sort of thing happens, do I? You people do, your people do. I know that, you know that."[1] Amidst a string of "you" and "I"s, Perot had destroyed the familiarity he sought to build. The word kept sabotaging his quest for rhetorical kinship. "Now good, decent people all over this country, and particularly your folks, have got bars on the windows and bars on the doors. . . ." Crime and the use of drugs "is absolutely devastating to our country and absolutely devastating to you and your people."[2] "Correct it!," a man in the audience shouted after hearing the exclusionary language. But Perot went on, apparently not realizing that even a hint of separatism was enough to increase suspicions about his southern roots. Potential presidents must enact their roles in the collective "we" rather than exclusive "I."

Rarely in that year had any politician failed so publicly and completely to match intentions with the rhetorical requirements of a setting. One of the delegates noted that "people in the audience were beginning to get very frustrated."[3] And evening news reports focused on the gaff as the only significant news in Perot's appearance before the NAACP.[4]

Kenneth Burke has noted that "identification is compensatory to division."[5] We expect that we can use our rhetorical skills to close unwanted gaps between ourselves and others. But the Texas billionaire's efforts represent a case of *misidentification.* He raised doubts when he sought to reassure. His statements of association produced the opposite of their intended effects.

Like Perot, we are all supplicants. In large and sometimes small ways we search for the rhetorical resources that will help us secure our place in the lives of others. However tenuously our narratives are construed, we know that in some ways they must pass through the audience's world. If I want to claim kinship with others that I venerate, I want them to accept that kinship as legitimate. In a conversation about grade schools, I want to "share" stories about surviving 7th grade. Among the divorced, I want others to recognize in their experiences my own sense of loss and anger. With others who have seen their children successfully grow into adulthood, I want to collectively revisit parenthood's triumphs and traumas. I want an endorsement of my claim to group membership that such shared experiences imply.

While it is usually assumed that we can meet the expectations of others and narrow the gap that separates us, our best attempts are sometimes stillborn for a variety of reasons. Some messages fail to bridge individual differences because they are simply inept. In this mode, which could be called the Dan Quayle effect, the more a person says by way of attempted ingratiation, the less we "affiliate" with who they are or what they have to say.[6] When Dan Quayle attempted to quote the United Negro College Fund's slogan at their own meeting in 1989—"A mind is a terrible thing to waste"—a mutant form came out as an unintended parody. "What a waste it is to lose one's mind," he proudly declared to the puzzled group.[7]

Other messages ask for a level of knowledge or experience that exceeds the capability of an audience. These statements seek empathy from those who—for whatever reasons—lack the capacity to give it. Dmitri Shostakovich ostensibly wrote his 7th Symphony as an elegy to his own city of Leningrad, which barely survived two horrific years under relentless attack from the Nazis. This piece comes with its wartime setting as a stable rhetorical platform. When it was first performed in Philadelphia, one critic marveled at the sight of the "fur-clad, swank audience of Main-Line matrons" who were in attendance and stood for the playing of the *Internationale* as a gesture of solidarity before the symphony's performance.[8] But what could a socialist hymn ("Arise, ye prisoner of starvation!") possibly say to them? And could any of the well-fed concert-goers tap into their own experiential resources to make sense of the melancholy and desolation conveyed in Shostokovich's middle movements?

And finally, in rare instances a rhetor may seek the *appearance* of misidentification for the value it has as its own message of alienation. Ted Windt's analysis of the "diatribe" as a rhetorical form used by the Greek Cynics and adopted by contemporary dissenters points out the logic of a rhetoric of offense. "Cynics attacked basic societal values to which conventional speakers would customarily appeal," notes Windt.[9] Their style was confrontational and often deliberately offensive. Diogenes seemed to delight in testing the limits of Greek decorum by uttering nonsense, offering parodies of the powerful, and committing minor offenses (stealing and masturbating) as ways to make contrasts between minor violations of etiquette and larger social injustices.[10] The point, of course, was to shock: to force audiences to reassess widespread but fundamentally corrupt values. As Windt notes, this motive was reborn in the 1960s by iconoclasts of the counterculture like Jerry Rubin and

Abbie Hoffman.[11] But it is equally evident in the jeremiads issued by every new generation of intellectual provocateurs.

To be sure, many artists and advocates claim not to worry very much about whether they "connect" with certain audiences. They may argue that the problem of an unmoved audience lies with its members rather than the creator of the work. And they may have a point, if the universe of their own discourse is very small. A posture of indifference for the effects of our actions feeds on the romance of individualism. But advocates and public figures who are going to be judged and interpreted through the common conduit of news narratives can seldom be so indifferent. As Ross Perot and Dan Quayle surely understood, when one's words and intentions are subjects of broad public discussion, meaning and identification are all bound up in the same package of cultural expectations.

The focus on this chapter is on the unintended effects of disconfirmed identifications: some by design, and some by accident. The film *Bulworth* deliberately considers the rhetoric of offense, using it to elucidate familiar themes of political hypocrisy and authenticity. John Ahearn's sculptures of ordinary people for a New York City park raised unanticipated complaints from residents who wanted something more. And the Makah tribe of the state of Washington's Olympic Peninsula lost control of news narratives that cast doubt on the legitimacy of their decision to resume the ancient heritage of whaling. Each case illuminates different but interesting features of misidentification.

Bulworth's Satire of Political Manners

In certain moments, *Bulworth* seems to be a tale about the impotence of the Democratic Party in the age of Bill Clinton. And at other times—when it is at its most original and nutty—it adopts the unlikely medium of hip-hop culture to deconstruct the corruption of interest group politics.[12] The film belongs with a long string of cinematic jeremiads about the hypocrisy of the political self. *Bob Roberts, The Candidate* and countless others have functioned as reminders about the perceived inauthenticity of most political appeals. Indeed, the corruption of authority is a universal theme in all forms of narrative. Dramatists as diverse as Shakespeare and Charlie Chaplin have always found receptive audiences ready to explore the pretenses and darker regions of the powerful.

This presumption of the contaminating effects of power lies deep in the American experience. We cling to the romance of citizens as independent agents. And in this *mythos*, politics is easily marginalized as an impure substitute for the sentimental ideals of individual initiative and responsibility. Aided by the ascendancy of the political right through the 1980s and 1990s—with its imagery of small towns, the self-made man, and personal accountability—politics is usually portrayed as an unfortunate necessity. This theme of the politician as a plaid fabric of opportunism is so common that it is now a cliché. It comes with the assumption that the very process of political identification is an act of public betrayal. In that sense *Bulworth* is a fable particularly well suited to our own political agnosticism. Bulworth's reawakening of conscience is meant to confirm our suspicions that political rhetoric is a performance: an artful misrepresentation that smothers more authentic attitudes. But if it is conventional in the way it mocks the rhetorical veneer of campaigns and governing, it is more unusual in its generous tribute to black youth as essentially the only audience that fully appreciates the fake pieties of modern politics.

Warren Beatty's Jay Billington Bulworth is partly Beatty himself: a liberal Californian. But at the beginning of the film he wants to make the point that this senator has sold out, and is beginning to pay a high price. The film opens with the image of a candidate in utter despair. We see him sitting in his darkened office playing and replaying the hackneyed commercials that will be the basis of his reelection campaign. While the camera dwells on photos of liberal icons on his walls—Rosa Parks, Martin Luther King, Robert Kennedy—we hear the ads betray this heritage with talk of ending affirmative action, cutting government spending, and praising Californians who "live by the rules and pay their taxes." We are meant to witness the agony of a congressional liberal who has sold out to the centrist politics of his own party. Seven years of living with the constraints set by Republican majorities in the Senate and a Clintonesque "third way" have spent his idealism. Bulworth's crisis of conscience is complete. Suicide, it seems, is the only sensible answer.

This suicide wish is given a Hollywood spin that will ultimately give the film the source of much of its humor. He decides to extort a hack insurance-industry lobbyist for millions of dollars worth of death benefits in exchange for a favorable committee vote.

The lobbyist does not know that Bulworth has put out a contract on his own life, a far-fetched plot point, to be sure, but a fact that has a liberating effect on the way he will spend the next few days of his campaign. The apparent closure on his former life puts him at peace with himself. He has no anger or bitterness. There is no sarcasm. Indeed, he is downright cheery as he moves through a weekend of campaigning that is no longer constrained to pander to his own traditional political base. Like the Cynics of old, he will say what he wants, leaving increasingly desperate aides to undo the damage of his happy campaign of unvarnished truth.

The scene: a standard visit to a church in south-central Los Angeles, where we assume he will ask for support from the black community. A tagalong C-SPAN crew is assured by actor Oliver Platt's predictably edgy aide, Murphy, that it will all go "by the book." This and other events scheduled for the day will all be set pieces: familiar rhetorical moments where the candidate tells each audience exactly what they expect to hear. Of course that is precisely what will not happen. By the end of the day Murphy will have lived through his worst public relations nightmare, and the video crew will be counting future Peabodys as they collect tape of a candidate in total meltdown.

His decision to set aside the predictable rhetorical boilerplate about "a rebirth of democracy" at "the start of the new millennium" ends with an extended riff based on questions from the crowd:

WOMAN IN CHURCH: When riots and civil unrest went down about four years ago you promised us federal funding to rebuild our community. What happened?

BULWORTH: Well, what happened was that, ah, we all knew that was going to be big news for a while so we all came down here—Bush, Clinton, Wilson, all of us—got our pictures taken, told you what you wanted to hear, and we pretty much forgot about it.

(Gasps from the audience)

WOMAN: We can't get health insurance, life insurance, fire insurance. Why haven't you come out for Senate Bill 2720?

BULWORTH: (Cheerfully)   Because you haven't contributed to my campaign, have you? (Boos and more gasps)

You got any idea how much these insurance companies come up with? They pretty much depend on me to get a bill like that and bottle it up in my committee during an election, then that way we can kill it when you're not looking.

WOMAN: (in disbelief)   Are you *saying*, the Democratic Party doesn't care about the African American Community?

BULWORTH: Isn't that obvious? You've got half of your kids out of work and the other half are in jail. Do you see any Democrat doing anything about it? Certainly not me. So what are you going to do, vote Republican? C'mon, C'mon, you're not going to vote Republican. Let's call a spade a spade. (More boos) I mean, come on, you can have a *billion* man march. If you don't put down that malt liquor and chicken wings and get behind somebody other than a running back who stabs his wife, you're never going to get rid of somebody like me. (More boos)

The campaign is then off to a fundraiser at the posh home of the Lebowitz's in Beverly Hills, where the senator is supposed to ask for support from Hollywood's corporate leaders. He's late, and the guests are annoyed. But Murphy has done his job and partly mollified the group with a story that the candidate is probably working on last-minute changes in wording on "new guarantees" for the West Bank. They do not yet know that that their patience will be "rewarded" with a candidate who now seems permanently locked into the insult mode. Expecting a talk that will decry agitation by conservatives to "clean up" Hollywood, they are about to be part of a second round of verbal bombs gleefully tossed in their direction. Again, the fun of the film is in watching an "id" freed from its controlling superego; Groucho Marx in the body of a distinguished Senate eminence:

GUEST: Senator, do you think those of us in the entertainment business *need* government help in determining limits on the amount of sex and violence in today's films and television programs?

BULWORTH: You know, the funny thing is how . . . lousy
most of your stuff is. You know, you make violent films,
and you make dirty films, and you make family films,
and most of them aren't very good are they? Funny, there's
so many smart people [who] can work so hard on them,
and spend all that money on them, and make so much
money on 'em. . . . Why do you do this? It must be the
money. Must be the money. Turns everything to crap, you
know, but Jesus Christ, how much money do you guys
really need? (He laughs; they sit in stony silence)

GUEST: Just between us Senator, do you think it's advis-
able to schedule campaign stops with industry leaders
when you have such a low opinion of their product?

BULWORTH: My guys are not stupid. They always put the
big Jews on my schedule. You're mostly Jews here, right?
What . . . three out of four anyway.

GUEST: (in disbelief)   *Excuse me?*

BULWORTH: Look . . . (thumbing through the remarks he
was supposed to deliver) I'm sure Murphy put something
bad about (Louis) Farrakhan in here for you.

And so it goes.

The increasingly desperate Murphy is meant to remind us of
Bulworth's deviation from the political norm. He is what we assume all high-level staffers are: masters at placating constituents
and glossing over unpleasant facts. Our pleasure in watching
Bulworth rises in direct proportion to Murphy's obvious distress.
The bewildered aide is at a loss to explain why his boss has gone
off the rails, at one point demanding an explanation that will help
him fathom "the new strategy" of the Senator:

I'm concerned that you stood up in front of 300 people at
a black church and told them that they were not a factor
and never would be as long as we remain in the pocket of
the insurance lobby! I'm concerned that you went to a
fundraiser in Beverly Hills and told various leaders of the
entertainment industry that they make a lousy product and,
since many of them also happen to be Jewish, you decide

the prudent thing to do would be to mock their Jewish paranoia!

As an entertainment, *Bulworth* depends upon the spectacle of a role-type violation. The indignities the Marx Brothers visited upon Margaret Dumont in "Room Service" are not all that different from those imposed by Senator Bulworth. We know that daily life is ruled by expectations, and we are delighted to see them violated in the safe confines of farce.

But there is an edge to *Bulworth*. Beatty's point was certainly to do more than construct a comedy of manners. The shock value of the film owes something to the diatribe of intended misidentifications discussed earlier. It carries the old-fashioned American wish for a supposedly "true" politics of authenticity, and it does so by idealizing the freedom of a candidate who has momentarily broken free of the incessant temporizing that has become a synecdoche for the political process. The energy of the film flows from the Senator's momentary escape from his life in a dead political culture. Its bite comes partly from the fact that the victims of his calculated indifference to the requirements of identification are not just traditional targets, like the upper crust, but several real and significant power blocks who are not used to having their expectations violated for fun. We know the rules well. You can't say those things to a mostly black audience, or to a group of wealthy Hollywood executives who happen to be Jewish.

The film also carries another message, which Beatty may not have intended. Exposing one's own motives and calculations without modifications imposed by our internal censor reveal us as the politicians that we really are. Aristotle long ago noted that political impulses are embedded in our civility and social nature. To speak in "unvarnished truths"—even if it were possible—leaves us to pick up the pieces of misidentification. Beyond the humor of offended sensibilities, *Bulworth* makes the serious point that we abandon the arts of ingratiation at our peril.

Art as Unintended Commentary

Sculpture artist John Ahearn is perhaps one of the least likely in New York's art scene to be accused of racism. For years Ahearn worked and lived on Walton Avenue in the South Bronx, devoting most of his time to faithful images of black and Hispanic members of his own community. Since 1979 he has built a successful career rendering life-sized plaster casts of children, street people, and neighbors. In more ambitious projects the casts are remolded into bronze or fiberglass figures, then painted. Like George Segal's innovative and prosaic representations of ordinary people, Ahearn's work shuns the traditional heroic images of representational sculpture: for example, the kind seen in the commemorative representations of soldiers added to Maya Lin's simple Vietnam Veteran's memorial. He prefers a style critics have dubbed "Social Realism." But unlike Segal, Ahearn is not even remotely political in most of his work.[13] And where Segal's art reflects unpainted but lifelike forms, Ahearn uses acrylics and oils to add body and facial details, creating what one observer has described as a "three-dimensional picture."[14] The results are often riveting creations—at once "lifelike" but enormously variable: what an observer might expect to see if a group of mannequins were allowed to register the accumulated experiences of lifetime.

His subjects are nearly always residents near his studio, captured in moments they would comfortably recognize as their own. Wall sculptures on the sides of buildings on two Bronx corners offer settings that are disarmingly simple. One called "Double Dutch," features two girls twirling jump ropes for two others frozen in mid-flight. The other entitled "Back to School" is a tableau of parents and kids anxiously heading off to the first day of classes. Few would have perhaps predicted that this white artist from an affluent upstate family would have ended up as a chronicler of the residents of the South Bronx.

At the behest of his assistant, Rigoberto Torres, Ahearn often moved his studio to the sidewalk along Walton Avenue, encouraging curious neighbors and children from the grade school around the corner to volunteer as subjects. As The New Yorker's Jane Kramer noted in her influential profile of the artist,[15] many were rewarded with gifts of the casts he produced, often unaware of the fact that by the late 1980s he was becoming a "hot" item for collectors and museums around the country.

All of this suggests that the charge that would come his way was a counterfeit: an empty complaint of a city official suspicious of the presumptive friendliness of a white man in an ethnic neighborhood. That Ahearn was not interested in idealized symbols of the community would be an additional cause of suspicion, and put the artist on notice that even the most uninflected representations of Walton Avenue's residents could produce unintended meanings.

In 1986 Ahearn had won a competition to complete several sculptures for a small triangle of space in front of a new police precinct station built at the Bronx intersection of Jerome Avenue and 169th Street. It requires a stretch of the imagination to call the simple concrete island a "sculpture park," but he took his winning proposal seriously, planning three figures that would be placed on concrete pedestals in the space between the elevated subway tracks on one side, and the station house on the other. The effect, he hoped, would be that members of the community would like his images and conclude that "finally, this is really us!"[16] He was hardly naïve about the drug problems, crime, and unemployment in this neighborhood. The 44th precinct had among the highest crime rates in the city. But Kramer describes a man who was casually accepting of the local residents, and generous with his time and work.

His choice of subjects for the three spaces were neither heroes or achievers, but two young men and a girl in the business of living their unremarkable lives. "Raymond," a lean young Hispanic man in sneakers, black pants, and a black hooded sweatshirt, is kneeling next to his pit bull. The dog is looking into the distance; his master has a downward gaze suggesting he is occupied with his own thoughts (see photo). "Daleesha" is a thin 14-year-old girl in mid-stride on rollerskates, the whiteness of her footgear contrasting sharply with a colorful Batman t-shirt. With her hair in a topknot and her legs slightly bent, she looks like any adolescent who has confidently mastered a new thrill. "Corey" is a heavy muscular black man without a shirt. A basketball is tucked under his right arm. And his left foot rests on an enormous boom box, which seems to clearly announce his presence on the street.

There is no irony or ambiguity in these portraits. Anyone passing through a northeastern city might recognize these figures as residents belonging to particular place and time. Ahearn's tendency to *represent* ordinary people rather than actively promote a mood makes it difficult to conclude much about their lives. It is possible to wonder why the older and shirtless Corey hasn't found more to

John Ahearn, Raymond and Toby, 1989
oil on fiberglass
80 x 42 x 18 inches
The Broad Art Foundation
Used by Permission

do with his time. (He was 24 when his cast was made.) But there was nothing in the images to suggest a judgmental intent or a deeper subtext.[17]

Nonetheless, a small number of fretful neighbors, members of the police, and several staffers at the General Services Administration thought the sculptures sent the wrong message. While they never became an organized group of dissenters, their collective discomfort would stalk Ahearn from the moment the three images were placed on their pedestals. It took him only one week to decide to remove them.

In a scenario fit for this identity-sensitive age, he had projected more to a few vocal members of the community than he had intended. Good intentions somehow got overlooked while officials searched for the phantom of a racial slight. Were the images confrontational and racist? Or were they merely a continuation of Ahearn's pattern of working with residents from his immediate environment? As Kramer notes,

> Some . . . wanted statues of Martin Luther King or Malcolm X, or statues of children in their graduation gowns, or mothers carrying home groceries, or of men in suits on their way to important jobs downtown—something to show the good side of the neighborhood to white people driving down Jerome to Yankee Stadium for a game . . . [But] A couple of black bureaucrats talked about the pain of the neighborhood, and about people like Raymond, Corey, and Daleesha, lost to the streets, and about what happened when white artists like John Ahearn "glorified" that loss and insulted *them*.[18]

Hence, the unlikely charge of racism. For Claudette LeMelle, a black therapist with the unlikely position of executive assistant to the city's Department of General Services, the images were "racist and subjective." "Raymond was definitely not a boy with Lassie," she noted. He dressed like a crack dealer, and the dog looked threatening. For his part, Corey was "too fat to be a basketball player." He was more likely just "hanging out," waiting for trouble to find him. And Daleesha? "More like death walking" than a normal girl. LeMelle objected to the fact that Ahearn's painted sculptures did not duplicate all of the colors that might be captured in a photograph. Apparently blind to the artistic prerogative to rework colors and mass, she noted that Daleesha and the others were "all black, no color, no hair ribbons, no pink, no blue—nothing."[19]

According to Kramer, Ahearn was more philosophical than defiant as he made the decision to remove the sculptures. He said that he had "respect" for his critics, and did not want his art to become a cause for anger at him or his subjects. "It's not my job to be the punk artist in the neighborhood," he noted. "If I've misread my people it means I've misread myself and my concept."[20] In the end, he seemed more concerned about not having the feelings of his three subjects hurt in what he felt was a struggle that would begin in earnest when the New York media caught on to the developing story.

The sculptures thus came down and joined others in an exhibit in a local school. Ahearn moved on to a bigger studio in a mixed neighborhood on the Upper West Side of Manhattan, and to broad acclaim and new commissions from other cities. If anything, his work has sometimes been cited as slightly "bland"[21]— a far cry from its alleged offenses at Jerome Avenue and 169th Street.

What went wrong in the sculpture park? How had earnest representations of authentic figures from the community created opposition rather than identification? For Heather Wainright the answer is quite simple. When Ahearn exhibited images of his neighbors in galleries and exhibitions, the portraits "were about the subjects not the artist." But in the sculpture park, *his choices* became the issue:

> Ahearn's decision to use actual residents as models and thus add a participatory dimension was positive, but did not alone discharge his responsibility to involve the "target community," because the three figures Ahearn cast did not merely represent the individuals depicted, they stood in for the entire community. The community understood this instantly, and were moved to action.[22]

Ahearn would probably not disagree with Wainright. He was genuinely surprised by the hostility to the images, sensing from the moment they were unloaded from the delivery truck that "the mood wasn't right."[23] But Wainright's suggestion that Ahearn had an obligation to seek prior approval from virtually the entire community seems unrealistic. While it is appropriate to show drawings or models of a work commissioned for a public place, it's quite another to ask that the artist involve the audience in the process of determining the subjects for a project. Committees are apt to give us the equivalents of George Washington in a Roman toga: absurd images created in a process of preemptive censorship.

What is so interesting about Wainright and Ahearn's views is just how overtly rhetorical they are. In both there is an implicit understanding that those being addressed have expectations that must somehow be answered. Ahearn sought to display members of the community to itself. He used art for identification just as I have defined it in chapter 1: creating expressive content that would encourage a "conscious alignment" of the audience "with the experiences, ideas, and expressions of others."

Those unhappy with the three figures saw them as somehow unworthy of their modest concrete pedestals. But identification is not the same thing as idealization. In contrast to the charge that the artist was somehow racist, a more plausible conclusion is that he placed more faith in producing a kind of egalitarian identification than his critics. Surely, he thought, members of the community would recognize their own. In an important sense Ahearn was probably not only the least racist of the lot, but also apparently free from the class consciousness that made his opponents not want to see public representations of ordinary citizens.

The class issue cuts deeply here. It is both the curse and blessing of "Art" that it is casually understood as the representation of the beautiful and admired. Institutional art clearly trades in its power to evoke what we want to believe about ourselves. The energy bound up in eulogistic representations of things or people is what funds exhibits, gets suburbanites into the city, and sells tickets for traveling exhibits. But of course in this truncated view, Raymond, Corey, and Daleesha were bound to come up short. Neither their lives nor the setting for their images offered much that could be idealized.

There are several "what ifs" here that might have changed the tensions created by these images in the particular location of Jerome Avenue. Perhaps this misidentification was partly a matter of the physical relationship between the figures and those who would gaze on them. What if the three characters had been kept off their pedestals and simply occupied places at ground level? To have done so might have diminished the implication that they were somehow special representatives of the community. And what if he had stayed with child subjects? Many of his other outdoor sculptures offer less threatening representations of children. And was the setting of a police station the wrong place to put these images? Given the sensibilities of Ahearn's critics, men like Corey and Raymond are perhaps more likely to be detained in a police station than given a privileged position in front of one. In the environment of the city, men like these are often marginalized subjects of suspicion, a fact that was transparent in the objections of the women who sought their removal.

In the end, these or other changes might have not made much of a difference. As Kramer has concluded, Ahearn was "caught in the crossfire of other people's priorities."[24] They would invest the images with their own fantasies for the subjects, finding motives and suspicious intentions that could not be easily refuted by anyone, especially the three mute figures.

The Makah: The Troubled Saga of an Identity Symbol

For hundreds of years the small tribe of Indians that occupied a rugged coastal foothold of the Washington's Olympic Peninsula existed in a very private world. The vast reaches of this northwestern corner of the continental United States is an isolated landscape of mountains and clouds, cut off from much of the rest of the world by thick rugged forests to the south, and the watery coastline of the Strait of Juan de Fuga to the north. Prior to the annexation of their lands in 1855, the tribe had flourished by farming the cold waters of the Pacific for fish, seal, and whale. And after the establishment of the Makah reservation at Neah Bay, the tribe continued whaling until commercial operations from Alaska to California made the Grays nearly extinct.

At one point the tribe seemed destined for a similar fate. Over the years, many had left the reservation, and the fifteen hundred or so that remained did their best to make accommodations to life in twentieth-century America. Some worked in construction and logging; others relocated to neighboring Seattle, sometimes drifting into a familiar downward spiral of social and economic isolation. But two major and related events would change the Makah forever: the first enhancing the authenticity of their fragile cultural identity, and the second putting that identity to its most severe test.

The first evolved from a 1970 archeological dig at the abandoned village of Ozette. A crew from Washington State University worked with local residents to uncover a trove of whaling artifacts that established a twenty-five hundred year history of Indian whaling.[25] Many of those items ended up in the Makah's ambitious

Cultural and Research Center in the town of Neah Bay. The center has since become a tourist attraction drawing twenty-thousand visitors a year, but its larger impact has clearly been on the Makah's sense of place. The extended human history of Cape Flattery documented in the museum has established the tribe's ancient roots and given it a narrative distinct from the Anglo meccas of the urban Northwest.

The second event grew from that reconstituted identity. In 1995 the tribe announced its intention to begin whale hunts that have been "a tradition of the Makah for more than 2000 years."[26] With the gray whale off the endangered species list, members sought to take one of the defining features of their past out of the museum and back into the present. To Micah McCarty, who became the whaling crew's most eloquent member, it was a chance to make a bridge to the past. "I'm the last living will and testament of my ancestors," he noted. The act of whaling was a way to connect with them while denying the prospect of "dying on the job in some industrial reality."[27]

The importance of whaling is explained in the text that accompanies an exhibit in the Makah museum:

> While the Makah were noted for their ability as fishermen and seal hunters, they were probably most noted for their exploits as whale hunters. More than anything else, whale hunting utilized almost every technical skill possessed by the Makahs from the building of the canoes, to the development of the equipment, the intense physical training, the fulfillment of spiritual preparations for the hunt, and extraordinary knowledge of the ocean. The whaling canoe holds a crew of eight men with each man having a specific task to perform throughout the entire whale hunt. Once the whale was harpooned, float bags made of hair seal skins were attached to the harpoon line and were thrown into the water as a means of tiring the whale. The actual killing of the whale was done by a special lance. Once this was done, a man dove into the water and sewed the whale's mouth shut to help prevent the whale from sinking after he was dead. The whale was then towed ashore and was divided among the people of the village. More than anything else, the whale hunt represented the ultimate in both physical and spiritual preparedness and the wealth of the Makah Indian culture.[28]

To begin whaling even on a very small scale, the Makah had to satisfy the International Whaling Commission (IWC) that it had a significant and unmet need to slaughter one of these magnificent thirty-ton mammals. And that need required a rhetoric of mortification essentially outlining the tribe's violation of its heritage. To some members of the tribe, whaling was a "cultural necessity."

> Many of our tribal members feel that our health problems result from the loss of our traditional seafood and sea-mammal diet. . . . We also believe that the problems that are troubling our young people stem from lack of discipline and pride and we hope that the restoration of whaling will help restore that. But we also want to fulfill the legacy of our forefathers and restore a part of our culture that was taken from us.[29]

But the Makah must have sense that they would not have the only word on an act intended to reconstitute their identity. The intention to begin whaling again after an eighty-year absence was an invitation to others—especially to millions on the West coast—who had constructed their own *mythos* surrounding the re-emergence of the gray whale in the waters of the Pacific. It set up a contest that would produce what Burke has described as identification based on "antithesis:" the objectives of the tribe drew millions of others together in united opposition.[30]

As the IWC's approval of the Makah's request surfaced in Seattle's media, a second counternarrative of whale protection emerged. For the Makah the whale hunt was a source of its redemption. But for many others, identification with the increasingly robust population of living whales was a source of pride. A "Save the Whales" bumper sticker might be a cultural cliché, but its very obviousness points to its place as an ultimate term: the assertion of an unchallengable social good. The impulse to protect whales from hunts is now deeply woven into the fabric of contemporary American life. Prior to the hunt a flood of letters poured into Seattle's two major newspapers, with those in opposition outnumbering supporters of the hunt ten to one.[31]

Such a measure is obviously inadequate as an objective reflection of public opinion. But it is clear that many residents in the Puget Sound region were unhappy with what they saw. And many reflected the self-reflexive environmentalism of Paul Watson of the Sea Shepherd Society, who placed whales and other sea animals in the same interconnected web of life.

> If we can't save those sentient families of cetaceans, these magnificent intelligent and gentle creatures, then what hope do we have of saving the sea turtle, the salmon, the lobster, the plankton? What hope do we have of saving ourselves?[32]

Others argued that the hunt was an illegitimate attempt by the tribe to claim a separateness from the larger culture. The implication was that the tribe had been conveniently selective in deciding how it would reclaim its identity. As one letter-writer noted in the *Seattle Times*:

> Michael McCarty, a Makah, was quoted as saying, "Harpooning, going back to the old days is just awesome for the whole tribe." Wouldn't it be even more "awesome" to really go back to the "old days?" Make your clothing on looms so you will look like your ancestors when you are hunting. Give up Gore-Tex and Thinsulate, wear moccasins instead of sneakers and hiking boots. Grow and hunt the rest of your food, stop going to grocery stores. Stop using electricity and all the appliances it supplies.... Stop living in modern-day homes and live in lodges like your forefathers.... If you really want to return to the "old days" of your culture, then turn around and go all the way back."[33]

For anthropologist Patricia Erikson the increasingly vocal battle raised basic questions about how group symbols are constituted: "Who gets to control the expression of Makah identity—both its legitimacy and legality? [and] Who gets to decide what is 'cultural,' 'traditional,' or 'necessary?' "[34]

The war of words prior to the whale hunt soon became a war of television images. Seattle and national news outlets flocked to Neah Bay for the many weeks that the eight-member team of the *Hummingbird* and its support boats made unsuccessful attempts to kill a whale. With each effort the whaling crew had been shadowed by protesters in Zodiaks and larger boats, press boats, television-news helicopters, and the United States Coast Guard, which had orders to keep protesters five hundred yards from the Makahs. And each day brought more readers and viewers to the confrontations between the Makah crew and the protesters shadowing them. The goal of the more active groups was always the same: to scare away grays in the midst of their yearly migration between the icy waters of Alaska and the shallow lagoons off the coast of Mexico's Baja Peninsula.

News viewers would also come to know Alberta Thompson, a soft spoken tribal elder who opposed the hunt and had befriended a young Sea Shepherd activist, Lisa Distefano. One day in the fall when a hunt was still possible, Distefano manuvered her Zodiak into Neah Bay harbor at the invitation of Thompson, who had invited her to dinner. The press was a constant presence during this period, energized by the daily round of taunts between young men on the shore, and protesters in kayaks and boats just a few yards offshore. They would also record the scene of Distefano climbing onto the tribal dock, only to be pushed into the water by a resident caught up in the anger of the moment. In a frenzy of coverage that followed, tribal police handcuffed and arrested Distefano, while a large gathering of Neah Bay residents dragged her damaged Zodiak out of the water and triumphantly planted the tribal flag on it. In tight close-up, Thompson's grandmotherly face bore the sorrow of the moment and probably did further damage to the Makah cause.

During the spring hunt that would finally kill a female thirty-two-ton whale, most of the protester's boats were gone, confiscated in the previous days and weeks by the Coast Guard. In a telling sidebar to the story, local residents would come to realize that distrusted federal agencies in the form of the Guard and the National Marine Fisheries Service were actively intervening to help the hunt proceed. The Guard slowly but consistently put protesters out of business. And the Fisheries Service—according to some news reports—helped the tribe scout grays in the area. Agencies that were often criticized for policing and restricting sports fishermen were now perceived by many Anglo residents as granting special protections to Indian groups.

Even without access to waters immediately around the hunters, the press used news and traffic helicopters to cover the pursuit, broadcasting much of it live to Seattle. And for many it was an unsettling sight. In denial of representations by the tribe that the hunt was the continuation of an ancient ritual, the pictures relayed back to the rest of the nation seemed to communicate no profound moment of tribal rebirth. In these waters whales do not fear boats and make no attempt to evade humans. The high-speed Makah fishing boat that led the flotilla furiously circled the placid gray so that a tribal marksman could take aim on its massive skull. From the air its full size was clearly evident in the transparent sea, as was the red pool that quickly formed as it slowly rolled on its side. Amidst a tangle of lines and buoys, its slow-motion death defied the Moby Dick legend. The only frantic movement was from the crew in the lead powerboat, and a larger fishing vessel that would eventually haul the animal back to Neah Bay.

As Robert Sullivan has noted, it was an unusual "collision of events" that pitted "underwater instinctual mammalian migration" with an equally insistent "man-based need to define itself."[35] In the process, residents of Seattle became spectators to the death of a cherished symbol: a living creature that for many had become an object of cathartic identification. And two competing narratives offered very different impressions. A narrative of tradition argued by the Makahs was often eclipsed by a second that denied the tribe its preservationist past. Somehow—and perhaps unfairly—the tribal hunters had been turned into an image they never wanted: cowboys out to exploit a precious resource.

Earlier in the year one of the members of the crew noted wistfully that "After we hunt the whale we can pretty much go anywhere we want in the world, like on tours and stuff."[36] Little did they know that their notoriety on local television would sometimes make it difficult to even be served in a Seattle restaurant: one of the many unintended effects of this misidentification.

Patterns of Misidentification

Because they are very different, all three cases suggest different lessons. *Bulworth* offers a case of *willful* misidentification. Warren Beatty's character knows the rhetorical offense he is creating. And we are in on the joke: a gross role-type violation intended to suggest the fundamental corruption of modern politics. Jay Bulworth has not lost control of his own message. He has gleefully created offense to make his point. The cases of Ahearn and the Makahs appear to be otherwise. They are more troubling because they have

lost control of the ways their motives and actions have been interpreted. Their unintended misidentifications demanded efforts to
correct and restore mistaken conclusions. But "fixing" initial impressions is notoriously difficult: a fact Ahearn learned as he tried
to answer critics who were comfortable in their opposition to his
sculptures. In the short term, at least, nothing the artist said could
counter the power of the initial judgments read into his art. Rather
than argue with his critics, he accepted their rejection and had the
sculptures removed.

The Makah case raises several additional issues that touch on
the larger effects of discourse that fails to meet expectations. To
what extent should acts intended to restore the identity of a group
be measured only by their effects on that group? Or does the creation of identity require levels of acceptance and legitimacy in the
larger culture? The fact that letters in the Seattle papers ran heavily
against the hunt suggests that it was a rhetorical failure in the
region: a significant problem if one considers the Makah as seekers
of legitimacy in the larger culture. And there is every reason to
believe that they sometimes did. Groups can hardly function as
islands separated by the rest of society. Members of the tribe sa-
vored coverage in the national press. Members also allowed extensive access to outsiders, including Sullivan, who produced a
high-profile book about the hunt, and a German film crew preparing
a full-length documentary.

The distinction between group and culture-wide referents also
points to an important difference between identity formation in its
psychological and rhetorical forms. It is easy to imagine that one's
place in the tribe can be set without extensive reference to the
outside culture. In this sense, identity is "inside" and psychologi-
cally self-referential. Pleasing and confirming the expectations of
the group is enough. And without doubt, there was clearly a sense
of achievement among members of the tribe as well as other native
American supporters who had come to Neah Bay to celebrate the
kill.[37] The taking of the whale was not about money, noted one of
the hunters, but "about a great tradition. It's about calling out to our
ancestors. It's all about who we are as a people."[38]

In a rhetorical framework, however, one has to be concerned
not just about internal audiences, but external and accidental ones
as well. And it is hard to dismiss the importance of the external

audience made up of residents in the Puget Sound region and the rest of the nation. Discourse may be initially designed for its value as identity rhetoric, but the media machine of news has the power to magnify a message by projecting it to a secondary audience made up of millions rather than hundreds.

In the end, the event of the hunt turned less on specific events, than the ways the events were offered to others. Were the Makah rekindling a valuable old "custom," or exploiting a government "loophole" that granted limited whaling rights to Eskimos? Were they "hunters" or "killers?" Did they represent a threat to the recovery of the whale population, or did they remain the first and best custodians of the environment? And how does one begin to calculate the impact of pictures of the bloody whale and its pursuers?

Without question the actual story of the Makah hunt is misrepresented in such two-sided questions. The long chain of events preceding the successful kill was more subtle and complex. Some members of the tribe favored the hunt, and some opposed it. And others in the Northwest had their own diverse range of responses. But naming tends to force us into such reductions. And there is no doubt that the rhetoric of the Seattle media had primed its readers and viewers to respond along parallel tracks of opposition or support. In this sense, the Makahs faced the same dilemmas confronted by others whose acts are interpreted in news narratives communicated to the larger culture. In the misidentification of their words and motives they lost control of their own story.

Chapter 6

IDENTIFICATION AND COMMITMENT IN CIVIC CULTURE

Every nation's nationalism is the search for a principle that distinguishes insiders from outsiders and elevates the former over the latter.
—Todd Gitlin, *The Twilight of Common Dreams*

His country was built with words, and for a little time, while he talked, he lived there.
—Mary Cantwell, *Manhattan Memoir*

To many observers beyond its borders, the idea of Canada must sometimes seem like an implausibility. As a former Prime Minister once observed, the sprawling nation has too much geography and not enough history.[1] And therein lies its dilemma. A relatively small population of thirty-one million people live in a necklace of a half-dozen cities spread along its thirty-four hundred-mile border with the United States. The residents of Vancouver, Calgary, and Toronto share a proximity and outlook on life that often has more in common with their American neighbors to the south than their distant compatriots at the far ends of the continent. Most of the television shows and films Canadians see are American.[2] Magazines and books from American authors dominate the top-seller lists. And economic and trade policies are designed to accommodate the gigantic U.S. economy to which Canada is partly dependent. The premier of Ontario recently told an American audience that "What happens in Newfoundland and British Columbia economically does not affect us as much as what happens in Michigan, Ohio, [and] New York."[3] He was probably too courteous to note that the deference is rarely reciprocated. This quiet society has had to get used to the boisterous and continuous block party next door, where the revelers sometimes appear to have more money than common sense.

And then there is the country's evolutionary rather than revolutionary political history. Canada never forged a mythic national identity in rhetorical and military battles for independence, nor in a civil war that would give it a redemptive ideology to carry into the future. It has evolved from its British and French origins incrementally and without much bloodshed.[4] That it continues to struggle to gain ratification of a constitution acceptable to its confederation of increasingly independent-minded provinces speaks to its reluctance to use politics in the American mold: to impose a legislative outcome in the name of the national interest.[5]

If these factors were not enough to weaken the prospects for Canadian identity, there is the continuing question of the status of French Quebec. Fed by the deep passions of a linguistic culture war, the quest for protection of Quebec's unique standing has produced most of the political earthquakes in Canada's civil life since 1960. Leaders in the huge eastern province—which includes the largest metropolitan area in the country—have defined it as "different" from the rest of British Canada. Even the most accommodating of separatists insist that federal leaders in Ottawa recognize its "special status."

In a little more than a decade separatists nearly succeeded in creating an independent state. The Meech Lake Accord of 1990 would have granted special status to Quebec, but failed because of an eleventh-hour revolt of provincial leaders who needed to sign on. And a 1995 referendum on independence for Quebec was defeated by the province's citizens with just a 50.6 percent margin. Half of Quebec's voters wanted to move toward independence; half wanted to stay in the confederation.

In the new century separatism has lost some of its appeal.[6] But this continuing impasse has tested the patience of Anglos on the vast Canadian prairies, and the increasingly powerful Asian communities in the West. They have grown weary of these old battles, as well as the politicians from Ontario and Quebec who tend to dominate national politics. But even with these rifts, perhaps no other part of the world remains so agreeably civil and peaceful in the face of such profound geographical and political fractures.

My concern here is not primarily about the struggle to find Canadian identity, though it is a fascinating story, and provides a useful comparison to the American experience.[7] Rather, the focus of this concluding chapter is on civic identifications at the levels of the nation and the identity group. Among the many features of our self-definitions, we often include national identity as an important marker. As J. G. Herder has noted, it is in our nature to want to "feel at home somewhere," to be with our own kind.[8] Evocations of the nation represent what Robert Bellah and his colleagues have called "communities of memory" that "give qualitative meaning to the living of a life."[9] *They flow out of a sense that one shares a common homeland and culture, a historical memory, and a sense of common rights and duties with many others.*[10] By considering the macro-identifications connecting us to national and subnational groups, this chapter brings us to the end of a journey that started in the early chapters with explorations of microidentifications in messages.

Identification with the state comes with a range of costs and advantages. The goal of the first section is to explore its narrative, rhetorical and media mechanisms, with special attention to what the American and Canadian experience says for the present and the future. The middle of the chapter grows out of the first, examining the extent to which identity groups have replaced the state as sources of civic identifications. And the final section considers the declining possibilities for identification in the most iconic of American national symbols: the presidency.

In each of these sections two essential questions about national and group identity are addressed. First, have we evolved to a point where references to "the people" or the "nation" are—in Rod Hart's words—"faux identifications?"[11] This question tests the idea that the nation-state is partly a linguistic trick: an entity that makes sense in bureaucratic and geographical terms, but means less as a motivating force in everyday life. In Martha Nussbaum's words, identification with a state may be "morally irrelevant," because "it substitutes a colorful idol for substantive universal values" that apply equally to others beyond any political borders.[12] And second, does group identity now carry more rewards than national identity? It is easy to see transcendent appeals to patriotism and nationalism in times of crisis, such as the recent terrorist attacks on New York and Washington. But nationalism is not the same thing as national identity, and more peaceful times seem to feed forces for fragmentation that work against strong identification with the state.

Conceptual and Substantive Challenges to the Idea of Nationalism

A host of definitional factors make any discussion of identification with the state problematic. At the beginning of the twenty-first century nearly all simplified generalizations about other cultures seem reductive and incomplete. The rampant nationalism of the past, the rise of global trade in goods and information, and the melding of national political borders have all had their effects. Especially in the West there is much more sophistication about the permeability of cultural differences. The rise of the European Union and the merging of former communist states into NATO are important indicators, as is the international flow of management, capital, and workers across the borders of old rivals. The Japanese think of McDonalds as *their* fast food. And in an era of cross-border ownership transfers, it is now harder to identify the national origins of Volvos, Chryslers, and Fords.

To be sure, it has always taken a high degree of national chauvinism to think in purely nationalistic terms. Consider what is perhaps the most performed score in the whole classical music repertoire: George Frederick Handel's "Messiah." It is sometimes identified as one of the enduring achievements of English music, yet that label hardly suggests the variety of forces at work in its creation and performance. Handel, who was German, learned a great deal about composition during extended stays in Italy. He finally settled in London for much of his life, composing this masterpiece in a stunning twenty-four days. The work actually had its first performance in Ireland in 1742,[13] but today arguably no national group has greater reverence for it than the Japanese, who perform it with great regularity. My favorite version is a Swedish recording of a Japanese orchestra and chorus, with British soloists, all lead by a Japanese conductor trained in the Netherlands (Bach Collegium Japan, BIS-CD-891/892). In its original and modern forms, then, "The Messiah" has always been its own form of "world music:" a stew flavored by various national sensibilities.

To be sure, we could offer cultural artifacts that find their essence in one society: the intensity of spectators for British football, the Mexican fascination with telenovelas, the hero worship of Canadian hockey, the Scandinavian dislike of conspicuous consumption, and so on. But even these national traits work only as generalizations, not as descriptors of individual identities.

In addition to caution about assuming a tight linkage between an artifact and its cultural meaning, there are also compelling reasons to see nationalism as existing at the margins rather than the center of the individual's identity. For example, Michael Ignatieff has noted that the constant quest for the discovery of the "true" Canadian identity can push too hard. Like most of the rest of us, Canadians carry many other identities that claim a deeper place in their consciousness. Using a differential scheme suggested by Seymour Martin Lipset, he notes that they have a tendency to be more group oriented, mercantilist, statist, and deferential to authority. By contrast, Americans tend to be individualistic, antistatist, populist, and ideological.[14] But beyond these broad points this simple symmetry ends. Americans hardly notice these differences, he observes, while Canadians consider them and additional distinctions all of the time. To most Americans, Canada is that snowy realm north of the border that seems "a lot like home." To Canadians, a collection of distinctive differences offers some protection from the conclusion that they are just a satellite unable to pull free from a larger force. Such is what he calls the "narcissism of minor differences" that these tendencies matter more to the smaller power. The lesson, of course, is that cultural tendencies may be real, but they suggest essences rather than absolutes. A rabid nationalism that insists on an ideology of difference is likely to look distinctly quaint—if not dangerous—to many Westerners.

These are largely definitional problems, but there are substantive ones as well that must be dealt with at greater length. Most notably, identification with the state increasingly seems to be in competition with forces pulling from opposite sides. On one side the globalizing effects of media and mobility work against simple nationalistic ideas. And on the other side, communities that are immediate and local rather than national or political now seem more relevant.

This second force can be understood in terms of the rise of identity politics, which implies an empathy with *sub*national groups in which we see ourselves as stakeholders. In ways that will be considered in more detail later in this chapter, identification with a pluralistic nation-state has always been vulnerable to the forces of subnational differences. Women, African Americans, homosexuals, Japanese Americans, and others have been energized by revisionist histories emphasizing their own disenfranchisement from the state. In many ways, these communities have partly replaced political parties as the organizing agents for social change.[15] And their most fluent advocates have ranged widely in the ways they have explored identity and its discontents. Writers such as Sherman Alexie and bell hooks are a reminder that inclusive rhetorics of nationalism offer fewer psychic rewards than the passionate definitions of communities struggling to stand in distinction to the whole.[16]

The primacy of these communities is suggested at least indirectly in our withered faith in institutions that embrace the idea of a collective public: a pattern reflected educationally in the popularity of home schooling and decreasing interest in the fields of political science and sociology. But these indicators are only the tip of the iceberg. Measured in terms of the "social capital" of the connections we make in our own communities—tallied by Robert Putnam in terms of volunteering for governmental boards, voting, and so on[17]— active participation in civic affairs appears to be declining. Fewer Americans share an interest in elections, follow governmental news closely, or read a daily newspaper.[18] Presidents can no longer count on network television coverage for press conferences and speeches. And the same networks have largely abandoned full-time coverage of the old quadrennial ritual of the national political convention.

What gets our attention also seems to have changed. Health and financial news has gained a more prominent place in the nation's newscasts and newspapers, often at the expense of stories dealing with foreign and domestic policy.[19] Personal traumas have eclipsed the political as the currency of public discussion.[20] And because of the booming roller coaster economy at the end of the twentieth century, Wall Street partly eclipsed Washington as the place that establishes the nation's pulse.

In an age where the public life and its institutions struggle for legitimacy and sometimes for money, identity politics thrives as the locus of experience. Many of the five-million American members of close-knit Mormon communities, for example, share the same universe of values, attend to many of its official publications and broadcasting outlets, support church-related businesses, and contribute to it's six-billion-dollar income.[21] Like many other nongovernmental organizations and businesses, the church is an important surrogate/substitute for a larger society that can seem distant and alien.

The technologies of travel and media have also altered our sense of national distinctiveness. Like the citizens of Canada, the populations of Western nations increasingly occupy a polymorphous world that ignores political boundaries. It was perhaps no coincidence that it was a Canadian who coined the phrase, the "global village." If Marshall McLuhan's summation of the twin effects of a shrinking world and the internationalization of information is now a cliché, it remains so because it is true. Regional and national cultures are no longer advantaged in the ways that they were prior to the telegraph. The electronic media make distances insignificant, contributing to states of consciousness defined less by place and more by attention. Unlike generations just a hundred years ago, we no longer "live" in just one continuous time or place.[22] The media have become the psychic transports that old science fiction films promised, leaving our bodies behind while moving our consciousness around the world. Thus, the funeral of Britain's Princess Diana was witnessed by more people beyond the United Kingdom's borders than within them. And Hollywood's stars are as likely to be recognized as frequently in Prague as in New York. Revealingly, an Ottawa conference held in 1998 brought together culture ministers from nineteen nations to consider how to protect their own citizens from a tidal wave of American films, music, and television programming.[23] A nation's considerable distance from the American film capital no longer acts as a buffer of protection against the invasion of "foreign" cultural products.

The Reservoir of National Identity

Our sense of civic engagement may be uneven and highly changeable, but it is hardly negligible. We are sometimes moved to act on behalf of the needs of the state, or its local counterparts. Voting, writing letters to the editor, and serving on a local government committee, are typical activities. And many more participate at the more passive level of attending to the narratives of civil life. Identification with a state gains potency in the panorama of common stories that occupy the literature of the schools and the legends of adulthood. It can survive in individuals who have hardly visited their "home" country, as in many of the surviving nine thousand older adults who were sent as children from war-torn Britain to Australia in the mid-1900s.[24] And it can be enormously expressive, as was evident after the 2001 attacks on the United States.

Nationalist feelings are fed and replenished from this reservoir of shared myths and commonplaces. Outsiders may define other countries by their geography or borders. But their own state is best understood as a collection of attitudes captured in a repertoire of preferred narratives. In the United States these familiar stories range from young George Washington's cherry tree, to the mythologies of Lincoln's presidency, and onward through the shaky but surviving exceptionalism that still supports the interventionist foreign policies of modern presidents.

These national myths can be expressed in many ways, but three narrative dimensions seem especially obvious. The first includes eulogistic stories focused on past glories such as the American Revolution, the settlement of the West, or the defeat of Germany and Japan in World War II. These sagas of history have their own complex origins and revisionist alternatives. But most eventually get interpreted as affirmations of core values and basic beliefs. Nationalist feelings also surface in a second tier of narratives of national achievement. The landing on the moon, breakthroughs in business and science, and similar milestones are often used as representations of collective accomplishment. And in a third tier that seems especially suited to American meliorism, national feelings may be produced by events that symbolize reconciliation of differences and failures. The end of the Civil War, the assassinations of John Kennedy and Martin Luther King—even the bombing of the federal building in Oklahoma—can be given a gloss of national resolve. The details of some of these traumas frequently suggest the darker elements of the American character. But in the hypercompression of media storytelling they are often used to suggest that there are lessons to be learned and natural correctives that will eventually prevail.

This process of reworking traumas into myths usually takes years. But within hours of the explosion of the space shuttle Challenger, Ronald Reagan defined the preferred narrative of the American "pioneering spirit" in an eloquent tribute to the lost astronauts.

As "the nation's chief storyteller,"[25] he fulfilled his obligations to reframe the disaster not as a preventable failure of the space agency and its contractors, but in the familiar pieties of sacrifice and national honor. "We don't keep secrets and cover things up," he noted in an obvious rebuke to the secretive Soviet space program. "That's the way freedom is, and we wouldn't change it for a minute. We'll continue our quest in space."[26]

To be sure, national identifications created through narratives would seem to produce a very passive kind of civic engagement.[27] But in a real sense the state as a "good" or "just" society is mostly knowable only as a rhetorical construction.

Ideographs and the Production of Identity

Beyond a nation's stories, identity is told and confirmed in rich symbols and images. Following the paths of early surveyors of nationalistic symbols, such as W. Lloyd Warner, it makes sense to identify objects, agents, and narratives for their powers to evoke a sense of common experience. Warner's analysis of the floats making up a New England city's tercentenary parade offers a panorama of familiar identifications associated with war and sacrifice: references to the emblematic red poppy of "In Flanders Fields," identification of iconic warriors such as Abraham Lincoln, and messages of righteous patriotism.[28] The symbols are so familiar, and the intended emotional connections so obvious, that virtually everyone is capable of "reading" their meanings.

The point at which civic identifications are more subtle occurs when we move from representational symbols to discursive language: when words in a particular context recreate a sense of membership in the corporate state. Any society has a large number of terms that can function this way. They do so when they are in a structure that ties them to a shared ideology.

Michael McGee has called these words "ideographs," by which he means a cluster of words "related one to another in such a way as to produce a unity of commitment."[29] In essence, a given ideology becomes a "grammar" for interpreting a specific set of terms. Thus words like "justice" and "liberty" have multiple meanings, only some of which may offer strong associations with civic vices or virtues. The statement "He did justice to the song" offers no clear path to deep associations. But the phrases "with liberty and justice for all," or "give me liberty or give me death," obviously suggest linkages to the national political ideology. McGee's analysis is a useful reminder that, while ideologies offer a set of attitudes, recurring language combinations give them potency.

We get a glimpse of the difficulties facing attempts to define a Canadian identity when we search for a unified field of ideographs. For many Canadians the search for a clear national essence has been a continuing interest, and sometimes an obsession. "It is probably the defining characteristic of the place itself," notes Bruce Wallace.[30] In his own battles against provincial leaders trying to weaken federal authority, former Prime Minister Pierre Trudeau noted that the "people of Canada had to decide on their view of the country: Is a nation greater than the sum of its parts or is it a confederation of shopping centers?"[31] More specifically, what is the unique Canadian language for describing its past or expressing its miraculous normalcy? Is there a common language for its glorious geography? As Kieran Keohane asks, where is the "poetry of the nation" that will bind it together? Without it, he notes, quoting Frederic Jameson, there is no choice but to live with the problems of a society dominated by the micropolitics of in-groups: "a linguistic fragmentation of social life itself to the point where the norm is eclipsed" by private languages.[32]

Even the most basic ideographs can be problematic in Canada. For example, Coca Cola has used the Canadian national anthem in ads targeted to English Canadians, but has not used it in commercials broadcast in Quebec.[33] Similarly, the maple leaf flag is sometimes replaced by Quebec's fleur-de-lis at events with national significance. The fleur-de-lis often functions as a provocative counterstatement for the Quebecois, an icon of separation that is reminiscent of the ways the Confederate flag is sometimes used in the United States. Thus, at the funeral of the deceased hockey hero Maurice ("the Rocket") Richard, the coffin was draped in the Quebec flag rather than the maple leaf: a fact of evident dismay among supporters of the Montreal *Canadiens*. Was Richard a Quebecois separatist, or a hero for all of Canada? "I don't know Richard's politics, or whether he had an opinion on the matter" wrote the *Toronto Sun*'s Matthew Fisher, "But it's a fact that in the province of his birth the Rocket was either only a Canadian or French Canadian."[34] For Fisher either designation was acceptable if it included the "Canadian" marker.

Ideographs have value as expressive identifications. But they also have obvious limits as instruments of thought. Where the American founders promised the traditional rights to "life, liberty, and the pursuit of happiness," their Canadian counterparts offered something less prosaic in the commitment to "peace, order, and good government." One could say that the latter hardly represent ideas for which a person would lay down one's life. But to many Canadians that is just the point. Some would argue that American-style nationalism has had its day: that governments and societies are best understood in terms of the services rendered to their citizens rather than as providers of an essentially hollow identity. Many take pride in the fact that their national life exists without the jingoistic nationalism common to the military superpowers of the United States or the old Soviet Union. And many are quietly pleased with the fact that Canada has ranked at the top of the much-publicized United Nations Human Development Index, a broad measure of how well nations do in providing their citizens with high-quality services.[35] If Canadians lack as distinct an ideological reservoir from which to construct a rhetoric of national identifications, they clearly have a sense of their differences from the American character: differences that many clearly cherish.

News, Television, and National Identity

The two forces of national life that are widely thought to offer the greatest chances for an individual's alignment with a national community usually include news and mainstream television: news because it broadly sets a national agenda of concerns for public discussion, and television because its mainstream commercial forms are pervasive in every corner of the nation. Since one is a content type and the other is a more neutral media form, their effects sometimes overlap or nullify each other. But both share the same potential to address national audiences in ways that can register as relevant to their lives and experiences. My discussion here is limited to two conclusions that can be summarized in broad strokes. The first affirms the obvious; traditional American news formats—major newspapers, newsweeklies and television news—are often sources of continuing national identification. The second is more mixed. Even if its news content sometimes creates a national community, television's fealty to advertisers and a culture of entertainment ultimately undermines its potential as an instrument for civic identification.

To return to the first point: for reasons that are both obvious and unusual, the mainstream news media still primes its consumers to think in national terms. The same television networks that have abandoned live coverage of presidential statements continue to offer an endless fabric of news, information, and entertainment that ties us to what Horace Newcomb has described as our "expressive culture."[36]

Much of this output is trivial, but it still has its unifying effects. News in almost any form includes a daily tally of events that are best understood in the context of a national community. Major stories have their uses in offering platforms for carrying on a national conversation, such that we can learn to "care" about floods in the Midwest, plane crashes in Pittsburgh, or terrorist attacks on federal offices.

This power of the news media to define a national consciousness remains in place because news organizations still function as *national* services. Since their primary clients are within their home country, they create a news product that mirrors the culture and its values. Thus, even though they sell their reports to many nations and have many foreign news bureaus, the Associated Press, *Agence France Presse*, or the British Broadcasting Company are best seen as reflecting many of the priorities and values of their home countries.

There is also an additional feature of American national media that doubles the potential for delivering a distinctly nationalist message. American news consumers are unique in the developed West for having little appetite for foreign news stories.[37] In contrast to many other developed nations, events beyond our borders hardly matter: a feature of American life that ironically feeds the excesses of American exceptionalism while creating a simpler national news agenda that is easier to "connect" with.[38] Major American dailies such as the *New York Daily News* carry almost no foreign stories. And while cable and television networks do more, there is a long term trend for national stories and news with a "softer" focus.[39] Even in the context of terrorism and its overseas connections, most reporting came from Washington or other *domestic* news bureaus. For the year 2001—which contained wall-to-wall coverage of terrorist attacks against the United States in the final quarter—*domestic* datelines dominated foreign datelines by a ratio of five to one on the major American networks.[40]

This pattern generally matches data on the preferences of news audiences. Pew Research Center studies indicate that—with the exception of war reporting related to terrorist acts against the United States or Israel—Americans have little interest in events beyond its borders.[41] Attacks on the World Trade Center, the explosion of the space shuttle Challenger, earthquakes in California, and the movement of troops to the Persian Gulf in 1991 all scored high as stories followed "very closely" by their respondents. But stories without a direct American angle—the civil wars in Cambodia and Zaire, the expansion of NATO into Eastern Europe, and the 1998 conflict in Kosovo—hardly registered.

Ironically, if news tends to be a way to identify with the state, the evolving nature of commercial television is now pulling us in the other direction. The structural features of an industry that once played a modest role in engaging Americans in their civil life now contribute to their flight from it.

For many years analysts described television as a kind of "electronic hearth:" a place to gather around at the end of the day to sample the national *zeitgeist*.[42] But the hearth metaphor was always more alluring than true. It made some sense in a simpler time when the three major television networks dominated public attention, and portrayals of the nation's civic culture established the *gravitas* of the three networks.[43] But with the proliferation of cable and satellite alternatives, and the network's flight from public affairs content, the presumption for the agenda-setting function of television has weakened.[44] Many popular options—sports, music and lifestyle channels—make it easier to avoid having to confront problems of union or disunion. Even with the nearly eight hours of television exposure that is now typical in American households, it is decreasingly likely that the medium will contribute to a national conversation about anything except the most onerous national crisis.

In smaller and more isolated cultures television may still be a national touchstone. Indeed, many nations treat their national prime-time schedules as extensions of their sovereign soil. No easier way exists to communicate the preferred values and narratives of the state. And many see Hollywood as a potential colonizer ready to Americanize their own prime-time schedule. The decision of the

United Kingdom to produce a television soap opera emphasizing Welsh sensibilities and language is a case in point.[45] That was a notable achievement with a clear objective of protecting a language that hovers near the edge of extinction. But, as Joshua Meyrowitz has noted, television's dominance on our attention hardly yields an extended sense of shared membership in the culture. If anything, television's determination to avoid any sustained presentation of any single "place" or point of view contributes to the modern fragmentation of experience.[46]

Our clearest sense of place comes form the sustained relationships—personal, professional, and political—we establish in a given community. As the dominant form of popular culture, television superficially trades in the same inclusive values. Its programming must be capable of playing in Portland as well as Peoria. And its relentlessly upbeat quest for acceptance is predicated on characters and personalities that trigger a superficial level of empathy. But true community is denied by its one-way nature, and by the need to make content "safe" for advertisers. This second point is especially important, and explains why television is so uncomfortable with the political.

Civic life gains meaning from discussion and debate about how a nation will interpret and enforce its values and use its resources. Choices enforced by Congress, legislatures, the courts, and executives obviously effect every corner of a nation's life. The richer the discussion of these choices, the better the eventual decisions will be. Are tax and social policies making us a "barbell society," with a growing gap between the rich and poor? Should civil liberties be curtailed to increase national security? Do corporations have any ethical responsibilities to others in addition to their stockholders? These are the kinds of questions that need the spotlight of public discussion. But they are sometimes not easily accommodated in the commercial environment of the medium. Among several well-documented problems are television's bias for people over ideas.[47] Ideas must be discussed in the analogues of interesting visual images. In addition, the need to deliver audiences to advertisers in a quiescent frame of mind frequently requires a level of disengagement that precludes sustained and passionate advocacy of one "side" in a debate. Thus, in entertainment, characters with deep ideological convictions are usually avoided. Television's master forms of dramas and comedies usually exist in a political vacuum. Prime time's dramatic characters typically have no political views, and are rarely engaged in any kind of social action.

In news and information, the result is often a zero-sum formula for news reporting: "balanced" rather than probing when the subjects include key institutions. This formula of objectivity bleaches out the passions of political argument. No single idea is allowed to be dominant or salient. At the national level presidents and their opponents in Congress are often represented as only half-right on any issue.[48] And every political candidate seems to come with a core message and one identifiable defect. They are often defined by their strategies rather than their ideas.[49] And their actions are deemed newsworthy only when they have attacked their enemies.

CNN discovered the commercial limits of conflict just prior to the Persian Gulf War in 1991. Debates about whether Americans should die in the Middle East in order to keep the oil taps open made advertisers distinctly uncomfortable, as did much of the network's extensive coverage. It was not because advertisers feared the presentation of violence. Rather, they were squeamish about purchasing time in news programming that reflected the consequences of a land war near Kuwait, including the inevitable pictures of body bags of Americans lined up in military morgues.[50]

To be sure, television offers a nation the chance to see itself as it wishes to be. But as an environment for selling, it cannot risk anything beyond balanced and simplified advocacy.[51] Even its traditional strength as the source of common experience has been undermined by the proliferation of outlets. Like the internet, its attributes are also its liabilities. More outlets provide more forums for diverse communities of discourse. But those fragmented options come at the price of losing common forums for the discussion and arbitration of national differences.

Our "Attachment to Marginality:" The Preference for Localized Identification

As many observers noted after the dramatic attacks on the World Trade Center and the Pentagon, the nation was "brought together" in shared grief, anger, and resolve. Such was the power of that extraordinary national crisis and the endless reporting of it. But as many of those who have long tracked the changes in the national character have noted, the long-term trend is probably in the other direction: toward a preference for exclusion rather than a common national conversation.

In his own trenchant analysis of the disintegration of the political left specifically and of American discourse generally, Todd Gitlin poses most of the key questions raised by the drift toward social fragmentation:

> What has become of the ideal of a left—or, for that matter, of a nation—that federates people of different races, genders, sexualities, or for that matter, religions and classes? . . . Why are so many people attached to their marginality and why is so much of their intellectual labor spent developing theories to justify it? Why insist on difference with such rigidity, rancor, and blindness, to the exclusion of the possibility of common knowledge and common dreams?[52]

Gitlin notes that there is an apparent lack of will to seek common ground among various groups—feminists, blacks, native Americans, gays, and so on—who once needed and sometimes received the support of enlightened outsiders. Now, he argues, there is less patience for finding the common center. By declaring some form of the feminist assumption that "the personal is political," many Americans seem to have found meaning in politics as an *affirmation of self* rather than a national consensus. Perhaps we have always had this tendency, only hiding it behind more altruistic motives.[53] But we have never been clearer in our desire to identify the malevolent forces at work that deny our rights to self-fulfillment. The injuries inflicted on one's group are—through ideological identification—shared by all of its activist members. Thus, the aggressive police attack on Rodney King in Los Angeles is an attack on all blacks. The Senate's denial of Anita Hill's testimony against a Supreme Court nominee is a snub to all women. And the brutal murder of Matthew Shepard in Wyoming is evidence of the deep vein of homophobia that still runs the length of the entire country. Identity groups derive enormous energy from their abilities to argue such cases as transcendent representations of personal struggles experienced by their members.

Robert Hughes believes the polarization of "us" versus "them" is so pervasive in American life that it has become "addictive." He calls it the "the crack of politics—a short intense rush that the system craves again and again."[54] Rod Hart is more explicit in assessing its rhetorical features, asserting that the current political landscape has seen the "death of communal language."

> In other words, a highly individuated discourse has taken hold in the United States, a discourse that permits nobody to speak for anybody. . . . An ideology of particularism prevails, and it censures all unthinking attempts to build cross-group coalitions. Language that is too communal . . . is used sparingly, and language that is universal . . . is eschewed altogether.[55]

Hart argues that communities are at least partly created through the identification of villains. In a variant of the Burkean idea of identification through division he notes that hate is "the handmaiden of community."[56] The essential rhetorical question is whether we still want to accept an American narrative that includes attributions of inclusion for leaders and national institutions.

A common history can be a potent unifier.[57] But one troubling sign of our preference for expressions of division over unity is what appears to be the widening gulf between the common memory of our collective past, and what that memory will probably be like in fifty or a hundred years. The rhetorical touchstones of our history have often been political, and have featured moments of reconciliation and national will: the American canon as reflected in the War of Independence, the Civil War, the unity of purpose during World War II, and the Civil Rights crusades. Each produced enduring texts expressing the reality or wish of national inclusion.

That no longer seems true. Prosperity has provided fertile ground for feeding illusions of individual independence, even while it has distracted us from the origins of our connectedness. We have convinced ourselves that we have conquered most of the demons of the past: communism, corporate malfeasance, civil war, extensive poverty, and so on.[58] If that is so, how will we write our future as a nation? Will our singular history of conquest over the nation's challenges increasingly yield to a future collection of histories: competing accounts of how those at the margins fought individual battles for civil rights against the darker forces at work in the larger society? David Zarefsky has reminded us that the "belief that one is victimized, that others cannot understand or identify with one's experience, balkanizes our public life."[59] And yet in this new century it is difficult to find convincing expressions of the common interest that do not seem empty and stale: a fact that is especially evident in our altered responses to the most visible of all civic symbols, the American presidency.

The Diminished Capacity of the Presidency for Identification

Observers often assume that a legacy of the Clinton sex scandal, and other presidential misadventures of our recent past—Vietnam, Watergate, the Iranian hostage crisis, Iran-Contra, among others—is a decline in respect for the office and the person. In this view, it is President Clinton's character defects most recently that have harmed the office, contributing to the abandonment of the older mythologies of civic virtue that presidents were meant to embody.[60] But this is only partly correct, and misses deeper changes in the ways individuals now connect and disconnect from key national institutions. Indeed, the office of the presidency has retained and even enhanced its formal powers.[61] What has changed is that its occupants are increasingly unable to establish a durable and stable linkage between themselves and citizens and the larger structure of the state. We know the president, but do not identify with him. We honor the presidency, but we do not see those who occupy it as measuring up to some of those who came before. In contrast to the widespread public acceptance of Franklin Roosevelt, Harry Truman, Dwight Eisenhower and John Kennedy, we have placed more distance between more recent presidents and ourselves. Broadly speaking, for many Americans recent presidents have not been *from* us, or *reflections of what we want to believe about ourselves*, but agents of the increasingly distant enterprise of national politics. Even while we sometimes register strong approval for presidential actions, the presidency is receding to the edges of the national consciousness.

By "identification" in this context, I do not mean a sense of kinship or similarity, or even moral authority. I mean *a sense of psychological allegiance* with the president that matches its cinematic equivalents described in chapter 3. In this sense we identify with a president when we see events as the president describes them, and conclude that the president's battles are ours as well. We believe we understand his (and someday her) state of mind, as well as the motives and moral justifications for his actions.[62] Leaders generally have this potential, notes Murray Edelman, because they objectify what we like or fear.[63] In this sense, presidential identification is not particularly subtle or complex. But it does provide an initial gateway to the political world, an important point of entry to the nation's civil life.

The presidency is the oldest and most idealized political linkage we have.[64] We are still introduced to idealizations of the office during childhood. And we come to see the best of them (Washington, Jefferson, Jackson, Lincoln, Wilson, and the Roosevelts) as carriers of the national will and destiny. But contemporary presidents have a more difficult and troubled relationship with the *polis* than the titans of the office who exist in our selective historical memory. At one level they are now more "human;" we accept them for the faults as much as their strengths. But they are also heirs to an age that deprives them the moral authority of the most honored of the nation's early leaders.

In asserting this claim of a diminished presidency it is important to separate ubiquitous presidential approval ratings from the idea of presidential identification. The measure of a president's standing with the public at any point in time is easier to tally than public identification with him. The latter is deeper and extends beyond support for specific actions. Thus, the last three presidencies of Bush, Clinton, and Bush Jr. have shared the same exposure to distance-creating forces of alienation in ways that have been partly concealed by their relatively high approval ratings. Both Bushes, for example, enjoyed very strong support for war initiatives: the senior leader against Iraq's invasion of Kuwait, and the son's actions against terrorist camps in Afghanistan and the Middle East. And yet the father ended the presidency as the son began it: in a general fog of deep skepticism.

A number of factors have changed the way we relate to presidents. First, the skeptical press and even former White House employees are now in the nearly full-time business of deconstructing the person and the office, making smaller what the writers and analysts once made bigger. To see the difference we need only go back to the more majestic presidency of the 1960s. Ted's Sorensen's 1965 account of the Kennedy administration confirmed and romanticized Kennedy as the embodiment of what we wanted to believe about ourselves. The elegy starts before the book's title page, where Sorensen quotes John Buchan: "He will stand to those of us who are left as an incarnation of the spirit of the land he loved." And it proceeds into the first chapter with the observation that JFK was a "truly extraordinary man" with the accessible demeanor of an "ordinary person."[65] Assassination made Kennedy a special case. But the library of the mid-nineteenth to mid-twentieth century presidencies is full of similar accounts of presidential greatness,[66] distinctly more effusive in tone than the library of their modern counterparts.

For example, one analysis of *Time* magazine's rhetorical constructions of the modern presidency from 1945 reveals increased attention to stories framed in terms of conflict and siege. Rod Hart and his colleagues note that *Time* now focuses less on the person than the office, and more on the president's challengers.

> *Time* now describes a government up for grabs, a far cry from the Great Man Politics that so long dominated it. Gone is the spectacle of the president on a white steed dominating a panoramic battle scene. In its place is Washington politics as guerrilla warfare-hand-to-hand combat, snipers along Connecticut Avenue.[67]

Even former staffers have adopted the official incredulity that has replaced older ideas of civic virtue. The figures range from David Stockman writing about an uninformed and unprepared Ronald Reagan,[68] to George Stephanopoulos's confessions of complicity in working for a president whose imperfections he "didn't want to see."[69] In the current argot of presidential politics, issues are about "spin," attitudes are the products of "triangulation," and legislative initiatives are undertaken by designing strategic "campaigns." No one can be ever understood on their own terms, and nothing is ever what it first seems.

Second, presidents are now denied the mystifications of a certain distance, even while the office retains its aura of power.[70] The Lewinsky affair offers a perfect example, with its uncomfortably frank details coaxed into the public realm by an overzealous independent prosecutor. As Joe Klein has noted, "It is entirely possible that the Clinton era will be remembered by historians primarily as the moment when the distance between the president and the public evaporated forever."[71]

The lost mystique of the office is evident in other forms as well. By one estimate, over forty films featuring a real or fictitious president have been produced in the last decade alone.[72] To be sure, some of these characterizations remain idealistic or heroic (*Dave*, *Air Force One*, *The American President*, and television's *The West Wing*). But a surprising number represent presidents or presidential candidates as flawed and calculating (*Wag the Dog*, *Primary Colors*, *My Fellow Americans*, and *Nixon*). The latter film features the embattled president played by Anthony Hopkins as the perfect brooding Hamlet. On one of his nocturnal strolls through the deserted White House he passes a portrait of John F. Kennedy, and notes to himself ruefully that "when they look at you, they see what they want to be. And they look at me and see what they are."[73] Such is the state of our own suspicions about presidential limitations and motives. Our fascination with the details of their now more public lives gives them a familiarity that denies them the perfection and idealization that could make them moral agents.

Third, there is some evidence that, even since 1992, the press has increased its coverage of character flaws as a dimension of political campaigns. Presidents are viewed as unusually driven men who are often impaired by their ambition. For the month of January 2000, for example, roughly twice as many presidential campaign-related newspaper stories included mentions or elaborate references to candidate character as compared to the same month in 1992.[74] Reporters more consistently primed readers to think about character as a context for assessing all of the candidates. Some members of the press were quite conscious of it, especially in the primaries, noting that it gave a surprising lift to "outsiders" Bill Bradley and John McCain, who challenged the eventual party nominees.[75] The extended Clinton sex scandal certainly played a role in the campaign, and was exploited by George W. Bush and others with promises to restore "the dignity and honor of the presidency."[76] Ironically, the battle over the legitimacy of his election only fueled doubts many Americans had about his basic competence: doubts that would be either resolved or hidden—depending on your point of view— by his administration's responses to terrorist attacks on the United States.

There are also multiple causes that account for the increased psychological distance between the occupant of the White House and ourselves. They include what has already been noted: the public's gradual but well-documented drift away from interest in civic affairs,[77] and—as was discussed in chapter 3—increased media interest in the "back region" behaviors of the president, especially but not exclusively lifestyle and personal choices. In addition, there has been a significant reduction of presidential access to the television networks for unmediated coverage of official acts such as speeches.

With regard to back region exposure, as David Halberstam, Richard Sennett, and Joshua Meyrowitz have observed, the line separating private and public behavior has been obliterated.[78] No personal detail is too small to have significance. One benchmark that indicates how much we have changed in our estimates of what represents "fair" press reporting can be seen in the coverage of President Franklin Roosevelt. His family was able to cope with the multiple burdens of his crippling polio and a severely strained marriage without extensive press coverage. Revealingly, he was almost never photographed in his wheelchair or being assisted as he moved to his car. And his negotiated platonic relationship with the First Lady was certainly known by many who covered him, but was not the basis of press speculation. Roosevelt certainly did get his share of criticism, especially after the "court-packing" episode in 1937. But the press and public conventions of the time meant that they could not stray very far from the political.[79]

With regard to the loss of presidential television access: while there is no shortage of coverage of the president, his presence is only as a player in the news narratives of others. Compared to Presidents Eisenhower or Kennedy, contemporary leaders are more likely to appear as actors in someone else's drama.[80] Their rhetoric is distinctly a minor part of most reporting. Over the last twenty years the length of sound-bites for presidents and presidential candidates has decreased in favor of stories that give greater weight to journalistic narrators weaving tales of Byzantine motives and strategies.[81] The narrator's point of view has come to dominate most versions of news. We hear much more about our presidents than from them.

In the end, then, we have a somewhat diminished presidency: an office with its constitutional powers in tact and even enhanced, but often crippled by divided government and diminished credibility. At times the office of the presidency seems to have been transformed from being a force for transcending differences to being yet another cause of division in society. The litigation of the presidential election of 2000 in the courts was only the latest in a long line of divisive moments. Against the older forces of social integration, including the eulogized presidency, we now have perfected the tools for social separation, including deepened skepticism about the possibilities of collective action, the development of a disjointed internet, the fragmentation of reading and television-viewing choices, the proliferation of identity communities, and so on. As a nation/community we know more about each other than we ever have. We recognize pieces of ourselves in the leaders that now populate the neighborhood of our national life. But this very familiarity has denied us the distance that is often required to feel a sense of psychological alignment. In earlier times we read guarded and carefully crafted stories of presidential power and statecraft. Now it is otherwise. Viewed at close range and through the prism of personal motivations, the office looks smaller, and we hardly notice the statecraft.

Finding Coherence: A Coda

As we have seen, the engagement of individuals in the larger realms of civil life has its traditions and paradoxes. Americans are like their ancestors and the citizens of many other states. They find meaning and significance in national identity. Words and images allow us to occupy a "home" that provides familiar settings for significant stories and memories. Fed by reductive histories and a steady flow of news, these identifications are still able to suggest the "common conversation" that lies at the heart of the search for national identity. Such shared awareness gives us a collective consciousness and, potentially, a sense of distinctiveness that comes with one's attachment to the values and events of the state. Canadian responses to the pervasive cultural forces of the United States have illustrated just how much is actually at stake.

The paradox, of course, is that the idea of the state is an old one, and must compete with newer exigencies. For many intellectuals the United States' epochs of national triumph—victory in World War II, widespread prosperity, hegemony over competing nations—are largely in its past. Indeed, even before it was over, confidence in the "American Century" of the 1900s began to fade under the globalization of economies and information, and in the inward turn that gave increased importance to the self.[82] Postmodern doubts about the capacity of any state to serve the social and personal needs of its citizens have been temporarily muted by nationalistic calls to combat terrorism. But the impulse to honor political and social movements that get their energy from group-specific identities remains. Indeed, it has never been easier to attach oneself to a "community,"—real or "virtual"—that derives its meaning and unity by its opposition to the state.

All of these forces are what make the current fascination with ostensibly low levels of civic engagement so interesting. For Robert Bellah and his colleagues, the United States is struggling to make a "culture of coherence" out of a "culture of separation."[83] As they see it, the challenge is to duplicate across the culture the positive experiences represented in religious communities and families. For Robert Putnam, the prime author of the civil disengagement thesis, there has been a significant withering of our associations to informal and political groups. The America of his influential *Bowling Alone* seems to be a place where families have increasingly cocooned themselves in their homes, separated and disengaged from their own communities.[84] An evening stroll through most neighborhoods confirms the obvious. The number of homes lit only by the glow of a television set is a reminder of how much this nation has turned inward: how tranquilized it has become by its most ephemeral forms of popular culture.

The idea of community carries the presumption of a civil dimension, and it always should. But unlike the Veteran's Day marchers who have noticed thinning crowds with each successive year, academics and cultural observers have been slow to fully appreciate the increasingly atomized nature of civic identifications that preference regions rather than nations, identity groups over the *polis*, and personal fulfillment over social action.

Perhaps American, Canadian, and other polymorphous states need to be considered as something different: as metacultures that have evolved past the point where they can be studied as single units. It may be the case that older societies such as Italy and France have the advantage in the form of a clearer public understanding that the culture is not the same as the government. But how Americans will accommodate the needs of the state against the impulse to find meaning in smaller communities remains an issue where the questions are still clearer than the answers.

And so we end at a very different place from where we began. Feelings of association with a state and its leaders are a long way from the more intimate associations that flow from more personal forms of rhetoric. But all of the messages and situations discussed in these pages are governed by the same constants. Whether the mode is a private conversation, film, or formal appeals to loyalty for a state, identification is still no more than a possibility. It may be an impulse tightly woven into our nature. But as the many examples in these pages have suggested, we often struggle to realize its full potential. Rhetoric derives its enduring status as both an art and a kind of sociology partly from its explorations of the resources of communication to awaken the latent experiences of others. That we can be surprised by what fails and succeeds is evidence of a process that is not easily reduced to formulas or simple rules.

We also assume that identification flows from a sense of similarity to others and their ideas. But as the Kenneth Burke and many theorists of the arts have noted, it is often more than that. Capturing a feeling or state of mind others already "know" frequently calls for more subtle appeals tuned to the resonances of form, language, sense, and behavior.

Sometimes identifications are so ordinary that we hardly notice. But others are so extraordinary they cannot be ignored. And it is especially their art that provides a window onto the endlessly captivating process of making acquaintances out of strangers.

NOTES

Preface

1. Quoted in Howard Pollack, *Aaron Copland: The Life and Work of an Uncommon Man* (Urbana: University of Illinois Press, 1999), 40.

Chapter 1

1. For a review of recent advances in understanding the processes of cognition, see Eric Kandel and Larry Squire, "Neuroscience: Breaking Down Scientific Barriers to the Study of the Brain and Mind," *Science* 290 (2000): 1113–20.

2. Richard Thompson, *The Brain: A Neuroscience Primer, Second Edition* (New York: W. H. Freeman, 1993), 390.

3. Ibid., 351–67.

4. Stella's paintings of the Brooklyn Bridge, for example, are mechanistic images of arches and ropes marching to their own rhythms, indifferent to the individuals who could populate its landscape.

5. Robert Jourdain, *Music, the Brain and Ecstasy* (New York: Avon, 1997), 413.

6. Howard Pollack, *Aaron Copland: The Life and Work of an Uncommon Man* (Urbana: University of Illinois Press, 1999), 463.

7. Kenneth Burke, *Counter-Statement* (Berkeley: University of California Press, 1968), 31.

8. Evan Eisenberg, *The Recording Angel* (New York: McGraw Hill, 1987), 43–68.

9. Chaim Perelman and L. Olbrechts-Tyteca, *The New Rhetoric: A Treatise on Argument,* trans. John Wilkinson and Purcell Weaver (South Bend, Ind.: University of Notre Dame, 1969), 413.

10. Kenneth Burke, *Attitudes Toward History* (Boston: Beacon Press, 1961), 267.

11. Aaron D. Gresson III, "Phenomenology and the Rhetoric of Identification—A Neglected Dimension of Coalition Communication Inquiry," *Communication Quarterly* (Fall 1978): 15.

12. Plato, *Republic* bk. 2 and 3.

13. Aristotle, *Poetics* 1451, 9.

14. Aristotle, *Rhetoric* bk. 1, ch. 9.

15. Ibid., bk. 2, ch. 22.

16. Ibid., bk. 2, ch. 2.

17. Ibid., bk. 1, ch. 9.

18. Annie Dillard, *An American Childhood* (New York: Perennial Library, 1988), 6–65.

19. In his study of persuasion in Greece, George Kennedy argues that commonplaces *(loci communes)* "played no part" in Aristotle's rhetoric. Kennedy points out that Aristotle focused more on *topoi*, or general lines of argument: a fact which is arguably true. But it takes a very narrow reading of the *Rhetoric* to conclude that the specific beliefs of an audience had no role in his general approach. See George Kennedy, *The Art of Persuasion in Greece*, (Princeton, N.J.: Princeton University Press, 1963), 102.

20. Aristotle *Rhetoric* bk. 2, ch. 13.

21. See, for example, W. Lloyd Warner, *The Living and the Dead: A Study in the Symbolic Life of Americans Part I* (New Haven, Conn.: Yale University Press, 1959), 112; and Robert S. Lynd and Helen Merrell Lynd, *Middletown in Transition: A Study in Cultural Conflicts* (New York: Harvest, 1937), 413–18.

22. Aristotle, *Prior Analytics* bk. 2, ch 27.

23. *Rhetoric,* bk. 1, ch. 2.

24. Ibid.

25. Kenneth Burke, *A Rhetoric of Motives* (Berkeley, Calif.: University of California Press, 1969) 56.

26. Ibid., 21.

27. Burke, *A Rhetoric of Motives*, 21.

28. Teresa Ortega, " 'My Name is Sue! How do you do?': Johnny Cash as Lesbian Icon," *South Atlantic Quarterly* (Winter 1995): 260.

29. Quoted in T. R. Reid, *Confucius Lives Next Door* (New York: Random House, 1999), 156.

30. Plato, *Gorgias*, trans. Robin Waterfield (New York: Oxford University Press, 1994), 463.

31. W. K. C. Guthrie, *The Sophists* (Cambridge: Cambridge University Press, 1971), 272.

32. Ibid., 21.

33. Ibid., 55–56.

34. See, for example, Karl R. Popper, *The Open Society and its Enemies,* vol. 1, 5th ed. (Princeton: Princeton University Press, 1966), 42.

35. Kenneth Burke, "Definition of Man," *Language as Symbolic Action* (Berkeley: University of California Press, 1966), 16. His full definition is in chapter 2.

36. See, for example, Dilip Gaonkar, "Rhetoric and Its Double: Reflections on the Rhetorical Turn in the Human Sciences," in *The Rhetorical Turn* ed. Herbert Simons (Chicago: University of Chicago Press, 1990), 341–66; and Hugh D. Duncan, *Language and Literature in Society* (New York: Bedminster Press, 1961), 103–11.

37. George H. Mead, *Mind, Self, and Society* (Chicago: University of Chicago Press, 1962), 253.

38. John Kennedy, *Profiles in Courage, Memorial Edition* (New York: Harper and Row, 1964), 56.

39. Richard Schickel, *Cary Grant: A Celebration* (Boston: Little Brown and Co., 1983), 145.

40. Mead, 253.

41. Ibid., 254.

42. See, for example, Hugh D. Duncan, *Communication and Social Order* (New York: Oxford University Press, 1962), 93–105.

43. Anselm Strauss, "Identity, Biography, History, and Symbolic Representations," *Social Psychology Quarterly* 58, no. 1: 4–12.

44. Sigmund Freud, *Group Psychology and the Analysis of Ego,* trans. James Strachey (New York: W. W. Norton, 1959), 37.

45. Sigmund Freud, *The Interpretation of Dreams,* trans. A. A. Brill (New York: Modern Library, 1950), 210–14.

46. See, for example, Peter Berger and Thomas Luckmann, *The Social Construction of Reality* (New York: Anchor, 1967), 173–80; Orrin Klapp, *Collective Search for Identity* (New York: Holt, Rinehart, and Winston, 1969), 1–37; Joseph R. Gusfield, *Symbolic Crusade: Status Politics and the American Temperance Movement* (Urbana, Ill.: University of Illinois Press, 1966); Kenneth Burke, "Dramatism," *The International Encyclopedia of the Social Sciences,* vol. 7, ed. David Sills (New York: Macmillan, 1968), 445–51.

47. Garry Wills, *John Wayne's America: The Politics of Celebrity* (New York: Anchor, 1959), 35.

48. Burke, *A Rhetoric of Motives,* 22.

49. Erving Goffman, *The Presentation of Self in Everyday Life* (New York: Anchor, 1959), 35.

50. Walter Cronkite, *A Reporter's Life* (New York: Knopf, 1996), 239.

51. Duncan, *Communication and Social Order*, 79.

52. Ibid., 80.

53. Jonathan Harr, *A Civil Action* (New York: Random House, 1995).

54. Robert Bellah, Richard Madsen, William Sullivan, Ann Swidler, and Steven Tipton, *Habits of the Heart, Updated Edition* (Berkeley: University of California Press, 1996), xi.

55. See, for example, Richard Sennett, *The Fall of Public Man* (New York: Vintage, 1978); Christopher Lasch, *The Culture of Narcissism* (New York: Warner Books, 1979); Robert Hughes, *The Culture of Complaint* (New York: Oxford, 1993).

56. Quoted in Burke, *A Rhetoric of Motives*, 50.

Chapter 2

1. The influence of Marx and Freud on Burke's output is enormous, since much of his work was completed at a time when their ideologies dominated intellectual circles. While widely adopted by many critics who see him from the frames of Freud and Marx, Burke has been often judged as insufficiently anchored in the psychological or historical determinism offered by each. For examples of the interpretation of Burke with reference to these perspectives see Mark Wright, "Burkean and Freudian Theories of Identification," *Communication Quarterly* (summer, 1994) 301–10; and Frank Lentricchia, *Criticism and Social Change* (Chicago: University of Chicago Press, 1983), 21–66.

2. Many became admirers or critics of Burke's output, including, Malcolm Cowley, William Carlos Williams, Sidney Hook, Max Black, Marianne Moore, Stanley Edgar Hyman, and others. For a collection of responses to Burke see William Rueckert, *Critical Responses to Kenneth Burke* (Minneapolis: University of Minnesota Press, 1969).

3. Dilip Gaonkar, "Rhetoric and its Double," in *The Rhetorical Turn* ed. Herbert W. Simons (Chicago: University of Chicago Press, 1990), 348.

4. Burke, *A Rhetoric of Motives*, 102.

5. For a useful review, see W. K Guthrie, *The Sophists* (Cambridge: Cambridge University Press, 1971), 50–68.

6. See, for example, Bernard Brock, "The Evolution of Kenneth Burke's Philosophy of Rhetoric," in *Extensions of the Burkeian System* ed. James Chesebro (Tuscaloosa: University of Alabama, 1993), 309–28.

7. Kenneth Burke, *Language as Symbolic Action: Essays on Life, Literature, and Method* (Berkeley: University of California Press, 1968), 3–20.

8. Kenneth Burke, "Poem," in *The Legacy of Kenneth Burke* ed. Herbert W. Simons and Trevor Melia (Madison: University of Wisconsin Press, 1989), 263.

9. Burke, *A Rhetoric of Motives*, 129.

10. Sheron Dailey Pattison, "Rhetoric and Audience Effect: Kenneth Burke on Form and Identification," in *Studies in Interpretation,* vol. 2 ed. Ester Doyle and Virginia Floyd (Amsterdam: Editions Rodopi N.V., 1977), 184–85.

11. Quoted in Ibid., 185.

12. Kenneth Burke, *Counter-Statement* (Berkeley: University of California Press, 1968), 48.

13. Ibid., 124.

14. Burke, *A Rhetoric of Motives*, 58.

15. Ibid., xiv.

16. Ibid., 55.

17. Ibid., 55–77.

18. Winans, quoted in Dennis G. Day, "Persuasion and the Concept of Identification," *Quarterly Journal of Speech* (October 1960): 273.

19. Robert T. Oliver, *The Psychology of Persuasive Speech* (New York: Longmans, 1942), 255.

20. Ibid., 266–70

21. Bernard Brock, "Evolution of Kenneth Burke's Criticism and Philosophy of Language," *Kenneth Burke and Contemporary European Thought* ed. Bernard Brock (Tuscaloosa: University of Alabama Press, 1995), 1.

22. Kenneth Burke, *Dramatism and Development* (Barre, Mass.: Clark University Press, 1972), 28.

23. Burke, *A Rhetoric of Motives*, 36.

24. See Burke's affirmation for the necessity of free choice in Ibid., 50.

25. William Rueckert, *Kenneth Burke and the Drama of Human Relations* (Minneapolis: University of Minnesota Press, 1963), 42.

26. Burke, *A Rhetoric of Motives*, 19.

27. This is a summary of a much more subtle analysis in Kenneth Burke's *The Rhetoric of Religion* (Berkeley: University of California Press, 1970), v–vi, 1–5.

28. Burke, *Attitudes Toward History,* 106.

29. Ibid.

30. Burke, *A Rhetoric of Motives*, 25.

31. A convincing case for the war as a watershed in setting up modern divisions in American political life is made by E. J. Dionne in *Why Americans Hate Politics* (New York: Simon and Schuster, 1991), 44–54.

32. Bill Clinton, "Remarks at Memorial Day Ceremony, May 31, 1993," *Public Papers of the Presidents of the United States, 1993, Book 1* (Washington, D.C.: U.S. Government Printing Office, 1994), 786.

33. Laurence Tribe, *Abortion: The Clash of Absolutes* (New York: Norton, 1990), 241–42.

34. George Cheney, "The Rhetoric of Identification and the Study of Organizational Communication," *Quarterly Journal of Speech* (May 1983) 148.

35. Christine Oravec, "Kenneth Burke's Concept of Association," in Simons and Melia, 180–84.

36. Burke, *A Rhetoric of Motives*, 134.

37. Burke lays out the possibilities for symbolic action in his discussion of the "pentad" (act, agent, agency, purpose, and scene), and the ratios that normally exist between them. See his *Grammar of Motives* (Berkeley: University of California Press, 1945), x–xvi, 3–20.

38. The distinction is Lentriccia's, 148.

39. Burke, *A Rhetoric of Motives*, 134.

40. Ibid., 134–35.

41. Ibid., 192.

42. Martin Luther King, "I Have a Dream," in *American Rhetorical Discourse*, 2d ed., ed. Ronald Reid (Prospect Heights, Ill.: Waveland, 1995), 780–81.

43. Analogical associations could also be considered as a process of producing a new "perspective by incongruity," by using one classification to cut "across other classifications on the bias." See Kenneth Burke, *Permanence and Change*, 2d rev. ed. (New York: Bobbs-Merrill, 1954), 102.

44. Burke, *A Rhetoric of Motives*, 135.

45. Oravec, 184.

46. Burke, *A Rhetoric of Motives*, 137.

47. Robert Hughes, *Culture of Complaint* (New York: Oxford University Press, 1993), 155–200.

48. James Davison Hunter offers useful summation of the discourse of these opposing factions, as it existed at the end of the

1980s, in his *Culture Wars: The Struggle to Define America* (New York: Basic, 1991), 144–48.

49. Hughes, 186.

50. Hunter, 144.

51. Madan Sarup, *Identity, Culture and the Postmodern World* (Athens: University of Georgia Press, 1996), 28.

52. Burke discusses a related but different point in what he calls "the imaging of transformation," where a single "family of images" might transcend two very different realities: for instance, when a poet bridges "murder" and "suicide" in to a common "ground" where both act as "terms for transformation in general." My point here is more psychological than rhetorical, focusing on the effects of these naming strategies rather than their design. See *A Rhetoric of Motives*, 10–11.

53. Hugh Dalziel Duncan, *Communication and Social Order* (New York: Oxford, 1968), 79.

54. This view owes less to Burke than a range of balance theorists attempting to account for the causes and effects of attitude change. For a classic conception of balance theory, see Leon Festinger, *A Theory of Cognitive Dissonance* (Evanston, Ill.: Row, Peterson, 1957), 1–47.

55. See, for example, Kenneth Gergen, *The Concept of Self* (New York: Holt, Rinehart and Winston 1971), 20–21.

56. Gordon Allport, *Becoming: Basic Considerations for a Psychology of Personality* (New Haven: Yale University Press, 1955), 19.

57. David Riesman, *The Lonely Crowd, Abridged and Revised Edition* (New Haven: Yale University Press, 1961), 25.

58. These are the words of an interviewee in Robert Bellah, et al. *Habits of the Heart, Updated Edition* (Berkeley: University of California Press, 1996), 77.

59. In both of these arenas two films come to mind: David Mamet's *Glengarry Glenn Ross* and Tim Robbin's *Bob Roberts*.

60. One classic attempt to define this kind of self-awareness is in Abraham Maslow's *Toward a Psychology of Being, Second Edition* (New York: Van Nostrand Reinhold, 1968), 71–114.

61. Joshua Meyrowitz, *No Sense of Place* (New York: Oxford University Press), 308–12; Christopher Lasch, *The Culture of Narcissism* (New York: W. W. Norton, 1978), 8–10; and Erving Goffman, *The Presentation of Self in Everyday Life* (New York: Doubleday, 1959), 1–16. All focus on the increasingly malleable nature of identity.

62. Wendell Harris, *Literary Meaning* (New York: New York University Press, 1996), 147.

63. Ibid., 142.

64. Quoted in Fred Friendly, *Due to Circumstances Beyond Our Control* (New York: Vintage, 1967), xvi.

Chapter 3

1. Howard Pollack, *Aaron Copland: The Life and Work of an Uncommon Man* (Urbana: University of Illinois Press, 1999), 13.

2. Bela Balazs, *Theory of the Film,* trans. Edith Bone (London: Dobson, 1952), 48.

3. Amy Barrett, "Questions for Tom Stoppard: Endless Love," *New York Times Magazine,* 20 May 2001, 23.

4. For example, Wayne Booth's analysis of "telling and showing," the use of narration and the author's "voice," and related concepts seem as relevant to film as to written fiction. See his *The Rhetoric of Fiction* (Chicago: University of Chicago Press, 1961), 169–270. For an overview of narrative theory and film, see David Bordwell, *Narrative and the Fiction Film* (Madison: University of Wisconsin Press, 1985), 1–26.

5. See, for example, Christian Metz, *The Imaginary Signifier: Psychoanalysis and the Cinema* trans. Celia Britton, Annwyl Williams, Ben Brewster, and Alfred Guzzetti (Bloomington: Indiana University Press, 1982).

6. See Teresa De Lauretis, *Alice Doesn't: Feminism, Semiotics, Cinema* (Bloomington: Indiana University Press, 1982).

7. Metz, 42–57, and P. David Marshall, *Celebrity and Power: Fame in Contemporary Culture* (Minneapolis: University of Minnesota Press, 1997), 13–14.

8. For example, Anthony Mazzella's reading of *Rear Window*—a film about which I will have more to say later—concludes that the story is partly about the main character's "sexual fears and anxieties." In this questionable reading, "The impotent L. B. Jefferies acquires power through his camera: the lens he uses for spying frequently rests on his lap and becomes the potency he lacks." See "Author, Auteur: Reading *Rear Window,*" in *Hitchcock's Rereleased Films: From Rope to Vertigo,* ed. Walter Raubicheck and Walter Srebnick (Detroit: Wayne State University Press, 1991), 66–67.

9. Jackie Stacey, "Feminine Fascinations: Forms of Identification in Star-Audience Relations," in *Stardom: Industry of Desire,* ed. Christine Cledhill (New York: Routledge: 1991), 149–55.

10. Ibid., 151.

11. Ibid., 149.

12. Cecilia Feilitzen and Olga Linne, "Identifying with Characters," *Journal of Communication* 25, no. 4 (1975): 53.

13. David Ansen, "Our Titanic Love Affair," *Newsweek* (online), February 23, 1998.

14. Hans Robert Jauss, *Aesthetic Experience and Literary Hermeneutics*, trans. Michael Shaw (Minneapolis: University of Minnesota Press, 1982), 152–88.

15. Marshall, 69.

16. This effect was considered in more detail in chapter 2.

17. Murray Smith, "Altered States: Character and Emotional Response in the Cinema," *Cinema Journal* (Summer 1994): 39–41.

18. Ibid., 40.

19. Ibid., 42.

20. Michael Korda, *Another Life* (New York: Random House, 1999), 478.

21. Smith, 42.

22. Ibid., 39–41.

23. Ibid., 41.

24. Brenda Cooper, "The Relevancy and Gender Identity in Spectator's Interpretations of *Thelma and Louise*," *Critical Studies in Mass Communication* (March 1999): 34.

25. Marshall, 68–69.

26. Jauss, 181.

27. Quoted in James Monaco, *How to Read a Film* (New York: Oxford University Press, 1977), 36.

28. See Robert Stam, *Film Theory: An Introduction* (Oxford: Blackwell, 2000), 148.

29. Ansen.

30. For a convincing rhapsody about the joys of discovery in even the most commercial of films, see Pauline Kael, "Trash, Art, and the Movies" in *Drama in Life: the Uses of Communication in Society,* ed. James Combs and Michael Mansfield (New York: Hastings House, 1976), 415–28.

31. Stacey, 148.

32. For an interesting case study see Todd Gitlin, *Inside Prime Time* (New York: Pantheon, 1983), 86–112.

33. Hugh D. Duncan, *Communication and Social Order* (New York: Oxford University Press, 1962), 80.

34. Monaco, 177.

35. Tania Modleski, *The Women Who Knew Too Much* (New York: Methuen, 1988), 73–85.

36. Laura Mulvey, "Visual Pleasure and Narrative Cinema," in *Feminist Film Theory: A Reader,* ed. Sue Thornham (New York: New York University Press, 1999), 66–69.

37. It is interesting to note that Modleski and Mulvey cited above do not see "Lisa" in the same way. Mulvey sees her as a largely passive object, but Modleski reads her as a more active agent.

38. For a somewhat different reading of the film see John Belton, "The Space of *Rear Window,*" in Raubicheck and Srebnick, 76–94.

39. William Goldman, *Adventures in the Screen Trade* (New York: Warner Books, 1983), 12.

40. James Surowiecki, "Hollywood's Star System, at a Cubicle Near You," *The New Yorker,* 28 May 2001, 58.

41. Kenneth Lynn, *Charlie Chaplin and His Times* (New York: Simon and Schuster, 1997), 458–59.

42. Alanna Nash, *Golden Girl: The Story of Jessica Savich* (New York: Dutton, 1988).

43. John Gregory Dunne, *Monster: Living Off of the Big Screen* (New York: Random House, 1997), 3–35.

44. Donald Horton and R. Richard Wohl, "Mass Communication and Para-Social Interaction: Observations on Intimacy at a Distance," *Psychiatry* 19 (1956): 215–29.

45. Ibid., 215.

46. For a discussion of stardom from a Marxist perspective see Richard Dyer, *Stars, New Edition* (London: British Film Institute, 1998), 126–50.

47. For a classic essay on the rise of celebrity, see Daniel J. Boorstin, *The Image: A Guide to Psuedo-Events in America* (New York: Harper and Row, 1962), 45–76.

48. Kenneth Hance, Homer Hendrickson, and Edwin Schoenberger, "The Later National Period: 1860–1930," in *A History and Criticism of American Public Address,* vol. 1, ed. William Norwood Brigance (New York: Russell and Russell, 1960), 125.

49. Joy Kasson, *Buffalo Bill's Wild West: Celebrity, Memory, and Popular Culture* (New York: Hill and Wang, 2000), 11–63.

50. Richard Sennett, *The Fall of Public Man* (New York: Vintage, 1978), 26.

51. For a sense of the hypocrisy of government explanations of the war, see Michael Arlen, *Living Room War* (New York: Viking, 1969), 6–15.

52. Todd Gitlin, *The Sixties: Years of Hope, Days of Rage* (New York: Bantam, 1989), 34.

53. Ibid., 31–54.

54. For an especially useful critique of the preference for inward authenticity see Christopher Lasch, *The Culture of Narcissism* (New York: W. W. Norton, 1978), 3–51.

55. Gitlin, 108.

56. Joshua Meyrowitz, *No Sense of Place* (New York: Oxford, 1985), 168.

57. A. M. Sperber, *Murrow: His Life and Times* (New York: Freundlich Books, 1986), 424–25.

58. *The White House Transcripts* ed. Gerald Gold (New York: Bantam, 1974).

59. Monroe's bouts of depression are now well known. Ashe had contracted AIDS, and deeply resented the intrusive press that made his disease public. Arthur Ashe, "My Privacy and the Public's Right to Know," speech to the National Press Club, C-SPAN, 26 May 1992.

60. Even the authors of *parodies* can be the targets of litigation by established authors or their estates. The California legislature has sought to give the heirs of celebrities exclusive rights to the use of their images for seventy years after the celebrity's death. See Robin Finn, "For Publisher, Book's Drama Spills into Real Life," *New York Times*, 8 June 2001, B2; and Rick Lyman, "Movie Stars Fear Inroads by Upstart Digital Actors," *New York Times*, 8 July 2001, 1, 16.

61. An evocation of public figures tied to a place and time is offered by Doris Kearns Goodwin in her memoir about growing up as a Brooklyn Dodgers fan. See *Wait Till Next Year: A Memoir* (New York: Simon and Schuster, 1997).

62. This metaphor is Meyrowitz's (p. 47), but it applies to a very large genre of "backstage" novels and films.

63. Quoted in Brian Lamb *Booknotes* (New York: Times Books, 1997), 140.

64. Blanche Wiesen Cook, *Eleanor Roosevelt, Volume One: 1884–1933* (New York: Viking, 1992), 224–36.

65. Max Frankel, *The Times of My Life* (New York: Random House, 1999), 230.

66. Ibid., 228.

Chapter 4

1. Gene Phillips, *George Cukor* (Boston: Twayne Publishers, 1982), 61–128.

2. Howard Pollack, *Aaron Copland: The Life and Work of An Uncommon Man* (Urbana: University of Illinois Press, 1999), 15–27. Of course this is a limited list of Copland's more accessible pieces. A good deal of his music is not programmatic. Appalachian Spring was written first as the "Ballet for Martha," and only later named by choreographer Martha Graham (388–401). And other important works (i.e., "Music for the Theater" and the Third Symphony) are distinctly more "New York" than "folk."

3. Neal Gabler provides a fascinating survey of the early studio founders. See his *An Empire of Their Own: How the Jews Invented Hollywood* (New York: Crown, 1988), 1–7.

4. Ibid., 6.

5. Brian Cox, "Audiences: Maddening or, Best of All, Mad?," *New York Times*, 5 September 1999, Sec. 2, 1, 5.

6. Elizabeth Giddens, "An Epistemic Case Study: Identification and Attitude Change in John McPhee's Coming Into the Country," *Rhetoric Review* (spring 1993): 386.

7. Ibid., 391.

8. James MacGregor Burns, *Roosevelt: The Lion and the Fox, 1982–1940* (New York: Harcourt Brace Javanovich, 1956), 203–5.

9. In fact, Southern presidents—notably Johnson, Carter, and Clinton—have been very progressive on race issues. But with some exceptions, that pattern is less apparent in the voting records of southern members of the House and Senate over the same periods.

10. See, for example, Lewis Paper, *The Promise and the Performance* (New York: Crown, 1975), 318–21.

11. Robert Mann, *The Walls of Jericho* (New York: Harcourt, Brace and Co., 1996), 36–38.

12. Ibid., 22–46.

13. The origins of Johnson's civil rights activism are complex, and rooted—as Robert Caro argues—in his compassion for the poor. For a detailed account of Johnson's racial attitudes see Robert Caro, "The Compassion of Lyndon Johnson," *The New Yorker*, 1 April 2002, 56–77.

14. Michael Oreskes, "Civil Rights Act Leaves Deep Mark on the American Political Landscape," *New York Times*, 2 July 1989, 16.

15. Robert Dallek, *Flawed Giant: Lyndon Johnson and His Times* (New York: Oxford University Press, 1998), 220.

16. It's important to remember that Johnson had huge cabinets of televisions in the White House residence and the Oval Office, one for each network. He was often glued to them. Like most presidents, he quickly calculated the effects of television coverage on the mood of the nation, and on the nation's judgment of his responses to events. Ironically, the same kind of "bloody coverage" that gave him momentum as he moved ahead on voting rights legislation after Selma would work against his policies in Vietnam.

17. Lyndon Johnson, *The Vantage Point: Perspectives on the Presidency* (New York: Holt, Rinehart and Winston, 1971), 161.

18. Ibid., 161–62.

19. Harry Truman appeared in 1946 to ask for legislation to end a railroad strike.

20. Dallek, 462.

21. Lyndon Johnson, "Special Message to the Congress: The American Promise," 15 March 1965. *Public Papers of the Presidents: Lyndon B. Johnson, 1965, Book I.* (Washington: United States Government Printing Office, 1966), 281.

22. Ibid., 281–82.

23. Ibid., 282.

24. Ibid.

25. Ibid., 283.

26. Ibid., 283–84.

27. Richard Goodwin, *Remembering America* (Boston: Little, Brown, 1988), 334.

28. Eric F. Goldman, *The Tragedy of Lyndon Johnson* (New York: Dell, 1968), 369.

29. Johnson, "Special Message," 285.

30. Ibid., 286.

31. See, for example, Paper, 79–80,

32. David Maraniss, *First In His Class* (New York: Simon and Schuster/Touchstone, 1995), 62–63.

33. Though the student movement of the new left was almost as fragmented as the society it criticized, the founding document of the Students for a Democratic Society, the "Port Huron Statement," provides a coherent overview of the reformist impulse of the times, several years before Vietnam mobilized more flamboyant activists. See *The New Student Left: An Antholog* ed. Mitchell Cohen and Dennis Hale (Boston: Beacon Press, 1966), 9–16.

34. Maraniss, 104–5.

35. Clinton was certainly sympathetic to many of the goals of the "counterculture," but it would be a mistake to characterize him as a dedicated member of the New Left. As many who have picked over the facts of Clinton's past have noted, he sought to maintain his "viability" within "the system," even while opposing the Vietnam War (ibid., 168).

36. Ibid., 200.

37. For example, Ronald Reagan—who is often compared to Clinton as a natural political leader—participated in a short student strike at his college, but the issues were strictly local. The strike was used to press reforms at a school that was near bankruptcy. See Ronald Reagan, *Where's the Rest of Me?* (New York: Karz, 1981), 24–30.

38. Maraniss, 213–14.

39. Bush quoted in Betty Glad, "How George Bush Lost the Presidential Election of 1992," in *The Clinton Presidency* ed. Stanley A. Renshon (Boulder: Westview Press, 1995), 15.

40. Interestingly, former Joint Chiefs of Staff Chairman, Colin Powell, notes that Clinton's draft record did not bother him. He writes that he "had worked in the Reagan-Bush era with many hard-nosed men—guys ready to get tough with Soviets, Iranians, Iraqis, Nicaraguans, or Panamanians—all of whom where the right age, but most of whom had managed to avoid serving during the Vietnam war." Colin Powell and Joesph Persico, *My American Journey* (New York: Random House, 1995), 581.

41. Denise Bostdorff, "Clinton's Characteristic Issue Management Style: Caution, Conciliation, and Conflict Avoidance in the Case of Gays in the Military," in *The Clinton Presidency* ed. Robert Denton and Rachel Holloway (Westport, Conn.: Praeger, 1996), 196.

42. Ibid., 211.

43. George Stephanopoulos, *All Too Human: A Political Education* (New York: Little, Brown, 1999), 26.

44. Philip Giraldi and Gordon Lewis, "Clinton is Not Welcome," *Houston Chronicle* (online), 31 May 1993.

45. Mary McGrory, "Fighting Stance Gets President Through Boos, Jeers," *Arizona Republic* (online), 2 June 1993.

46. "Reaction Mixed to Clinton Appearance," *St. Petersburg Times* (online), 1 June 1993.

47. Bill Clinton, "Remarks at Memorial Day Ceremony at the Vietnam Veterans Memorial," 3 May 1993. *Public Papers of the Presidents: William Jefferson Clinton, 1993, Book I* (Washington: U.S. Government Printing Office, 1994), 786.

48. Samuel and Dorothy Rosenman, *Presidential Style* (New York: Harper and Row, 1976), 338–39.

49. Johnson's private conversations reveal a stubborn man supremely confident of his powers of persuasion. This is evident in a conversation in which he insists that the reluctant Sargent Shriver give up managing the peace corps to become the administration's poverty head. See *Taking Charge: The Johnson White House Tapes: 1963–1964,* ed. Michael Beschloss (New York: Simon and Schuster, 1997), 202–5.

50. See, for example, Fred Greenstein, "Political Style and Political Leadership: The Case of Bill Clinton," in Renshon, 140.

51. Clinton, Remarks at Memorial Day Ceremony, 786.

52 Ibid.

53. Powell and Persico, 144–49.

54. Peter Cary and Fred Coleman, "Troubling Evidence on Vietnam POWs," *U.S. News and World Report*, 22 November 1993, 26.

55. Michael Isikoff, "Why POW/MIA extremists are Targeting McCain," *Newsweek*, 1 January 2000, 17.

56. Paul Richter and Howard Libit, "Clinton Cheered, Jeered at Vietnam Memorial," *Los Angeles Times*, 1 June 1993, A1.

57. Clinton, Remarks at Memorial Day Ceremony, 786.

58. Ibid., 787.

59. Richter and Libit.

60. David Gergen, *Eyewitness to Power* (New York: Simon and Schuster, 2000), 322.

61. Ibid, 323.

62. Beschloss, 202–5.

63. See Rachel Holloway, "The Clintons and the Health Care Crisis: Opportunity Lost, Promise Unfulfilled," in Denton and Holloway, 159–87.

64. See, for example, Stephanopoulos, 300–302.

65. Ana Puga, "Amid Boos, Clinton Asks War Healing," *Boston Globe* (online), June 1, 1993.

Chapter 5

1. Ross Perot, Speech the NAACP, Federal News Service (online), 11 July 1992.

2. Ibid.

3. "Ross Perot Rubs Some Blacks Wrong Way . . ." *Jet*, 27 July 1992, 5.

4. CBS Evening News, 12 July 1992.

5. Kenneth Burke, *A Rhetoric of Motives* (Berkeley: University of California Press, 1969) 23.

6. Steven Clayman would classify this as one form of a "disaffiliation response" in a rhetorical setting. For his study of such moments see his "Caveat Orator: Audience Disaffiliation in the 1988 Presidential Debates," *The Quarterly Journal of Speech* (February 1992): 33–60.

7. "Topics of the Times: Vocal Veeps," *New York Times*, 9 December 1992, A22.

8. Quoted in Christopher Gibbs, Program Notes for the 7th Symphony, *Stagebill*, The Philadelphia Orchestra, November/December, 2000, 41.

9. Theodore Windt, Jr., "The Diatribe: Last Resort for Protest," *Quarterly Journal of Speech* (February 1972): 7.

10. Ibid., 5–6.

11. Any list would be arbitrary, but writers such as Gore Vidal and Robert Hughes come to mind as critics who have cheerfully trashed many of America's sacred myths. See Vidal, *The Last Empire: Essays 1992–2000* (New York: Doubleday, 2001), and Hughes, *Culture of Complaint* (New York: Oxford, 1993).

12. *Bulworth* (Twentieth-Century Fox, 1998) was written by Jeremy Pikser and Warren Beatty. Beatty also directed.

13. Segal's "Depression Bread Line" (1999), for example, offers a series of bronze figures—features not filled in—that suggest the soul-destroying effects of poverty in the 1930s.

14. Robert Pincus, "Sculptures are Portraits of the Bronx," *San Diego Union*, 5 February 1995, D4.

15. Jane Kramer, *Whose Art Is It?*, (Durham, N.C.: Duke University Press, 1994), 37–132.

16. Ibid., 97.

17. Ahearn has been consistently praised for his engaging use of inner-city subjects. See, for example, Ken Johnson, "Art in Review: John Ahearn," *New York Times*, 25 September 1998, E35.

18. Kramer, 42.

19. Ibid., 90–91.

20. Ibid., 103.

21. Johnson.

22. Heather Wainwright, "In the Neighborhood: A Critique of Social Activist Art," *Public Art Review* (online), (Fall/Winter 1997).

23. Kramer, 97.

24. Ibid., 102.

25. For further background about the Makah, see Robert Sullivan, *A Whale Hunt* (New York: Scribner, 2000), 30–35.

26. "Makah Whaling: Questions and Answers" (online), Makah Nation website, 29 November 2000.

27. Quoted in Sullivan, 38.

28. Quoted in Patricia Erikson, "A-Whaling We Will Go: Encounters of Knowledge and Memory at the Makah Cultural and Research Center," *Cultural Anthropology* 4 (online), (1999).

29. Quoted in Ibid.

30. Kenneth Burke, *Dramatism and Development* (Barre, Mass.: Clark University Press, 1972), 28.

31. Erikson.

32. Paul Watson, "The Sea Shepherd Log" Sea Shepherd Conservation Society (online), 1 December 2000.

33. Quoted in Erikson.

34. Ibid.

35. Sullivan, 255.

36. Quoted in Sullivan, 133.

37. Sam Verhovek, "After the Hunt, Bitter Protest and Salty Blubber," *New York Times*, 19 May 1999, A14.

38. Quoted in Ibid.

Chapter 6

1. Seymour Martin Lipset, *Continental Divide: The Values and Institutions of the United States and Canada* (New York: Routledge, 1991), 56.

2. Colin Hoskins, Adam Finn, and Stuart McFadyen, "Television and Film in a Freer International Trade Environment: U.S. Dominance and Canadian Responses," in *Mass Media and Free Trade,* ed. Emile McAnany and Kenton Wilkinson (Austin: University of Texas, 1996), 75

3. Bruce Wallace, "What Makes a Canadian?" *McLean's*, 20 December 1999, 32.

4. This is not to overlook the long British efforts in the mid-1700s to subdue the colonies of New France, which included what is now Quebec and parts of the eastern midwest. Nor should later uprisings be underestimated in the ongoing tensions between British Canada and its French subculture. But as Maurice Charland notes, the *narratives* of Quebec's autonomy and domination have been the primary agents for constituting the *peuple Quebecois.* See his "Constitutive Rhetoric: The Case of the *Peuple Quebecois, The Quarterly Journal of Speech*, (May 1987) 134–47.

5. Even the charismatic federalist, Pierre Trudeau, fell short of complete provincial acceptance of the ever-evolving Canadian Constitution. Quebec still has not signed revisions put forth in 1982, a fact that contributes to a sense of national impasse. See, for example, Andrew Duffy, Randy Boswell, Carrie Buchanan, Joanne Laucius, Bev Wake, Christopher Guly and Laura Landon, "Flashpoints and Turbulence: Trudeau Leaves a Legacy of Controversy Over Key Decisions," *The Ottawa Citizen*, 29 September 2000, G10; Sean Gordon, "Fractures That Won't Heal," *Montreal Gazette*, 23 June 2000, A14.

6. William Orme, "After Seven Years, Quebec Has Lost Its Separatist Itch," *Los Angeles Times*, 12 May 2002, A3.

7. See, for example, Allan Smith, *Canada: An American Nation?* (Montreal: McGill-Queen's University Press, 1994).

8. Quoted in Ramsay Cook, *Canada, Quebec, and the Uses of Nationalism,* 2d ed. (Toronto: McClelland and Stewart, 1995), 224.

9. Robert Bellah, Richard Madsen, William Sullivan, Ann Swidler, and Steven Tipton, *Habits of the Heart: Individualism and Commitment in American Life, Updated Edition* (Berkeley: University of California, 1996), 282.

10. These are Anthony Smith's essential conditions for national identity in Western societies. See Richard Paterson, "Introduction: Collective Identity, Television, and Europe," in *National Identity and Europe,* ed. Phillip Drummond, Richard Paterson, and Janet Willis (London: BFI, 1993), 3.

11. Roderick Hart, "Community by Negation—An Agenda for Rhetorical Inquiry," in *Rhetoric and Community* ed. J. Michael Hogan (Columbia: University of South Carolina Press, 1998), xxxiii.

12. Martha Nussbaum, "Patriotism and Cosmopolitanism" in *For Love of Country,* ed. Joshua Cohen (Boston: Beacon Press, 1996), 5.

13. Peter Jacobi, *The Messiah Book* (New York: St. Martin's Press, 1982), 13–39.

14. Michael Ignatieff, "Minor Differences Mean a Lot," *New York Times,* 13 May 1990, Sec. 7, 41.

15. This notion of continued conflict is true to Marshall McLuhan's idea of the global village. He believed a shrinking world would not end international conflicts, but make them all the more apparent. See Gerald Stearn and Marshall McLuhan, "A Dialogue," in *McLuhan: Hot and Cool* (New York: Signet, 1967), 272.

16. These writers represent a huge class of interpreters of the minority experience in terms of a larger and sometimes hostile society. See, for example, Sherman Alexie, *Reservation Blues* (New York: Atlantic Monthly Press, 1995) and bell hooks, *Ain't I a Woman* (Boston: South End Press, 1981).

17. Robert Putnam, *Bowling Alone: The Collapse and Revival of American Community* (New York: Simon and Schuster, 2000), 24–28.

18. See, for example, "Fewer See Choice of President as Important," Pew Research Center for the People and the Press (online), 21 July 2000.

19. Doug Underwood, "Market Research and the Audience for Political News," in *The Politics of News* ed. Doris Graber, Denis McQuail, and Pippa Norris (Washington, Congressional Quarterly Press, 1998), 171–92.

20. Andie Tucher, "You News," *Columbia Journalism Review* (May/June 1997): 12–31.

21. Lawrence Wright, "Lives of the Saints," *The New Yorker,* 21 January 2002, 48.

22. Joshua Meyrowitz, *No Sense of Place* (New York: Oxford, 1985), 115–25.

23. Anthony DePalma, "19 Nations See U.S. as Threat to Cultures," *New York Times*, 1 July 1998, E1,

24. Janet Snell, "Walk in the Past," *The Guardian* (U.K.), 9 August 2000, Society Sec., 2–3.

25. The phrase is Mary Stuckey's in *The President as Interpreter in Chief* (Chatham, N.J.: Chatham House, 1991), 1–9.

26. Ronald Reagan, "Address to the Nation on the Explosion of the Space Shuttle Challenger, January 28, 1986," in *Public Papers of the Presidents of the United States, Book I, 1986* (Washington: U.S. Government Printing Office, 1988), 94–95.

27. Some have argued that passive media consumption of news has replaced other kinds of civic involvement, especially the critical analysis of what is reported. See, for example, Robert Entman, *Democracy Without Citizens* (New York: Oxford, 1989), 3–29.

28. See especially, W. Lloyd Warner, *The Living and the Dead*, vol. 5. Yankee City Series (New Haven: Yale University Press, 1959), 107–225.

29. Michael McGee, "The 'Ideograph:' A Link Between Rhetoric and Ideology," *The Quarterly Journal of Speech,* (February 1980): 16.

30. Bruce Wallace, "What Makes a Canadian?" *Maclean's*, 20 December 1999, 32.

31. Quoted in Duffy, et al., G10.

32. Kieran Keohane, *Symptoms of Canada: An Essay on Canadian Identity* (Toronto: University of Toronto Press, 1997), 4.

33. Peter Diekmeyer, "Should Marketers Fly the Flag?" *Montreal Gazette*, April 25, 2000 (online).

34. See Matthew Fisher, "The Rocket Played Hockey, Not Politics," *Toronto Sun*, 2 June 2000, 16.

35. Barbara Crossette, "Is Life Better in Bulgaria? It's a Matter of Perspective," *New York Times*, 7 September 1997, Sec 1, p. 4.

36. Horace Newcomb, "Other People's Fictions: Cultural Appropriations, Cultural Integrity, and International Media Strategies," in McAnany and Wilkinson, 93.

37. For the week of June 5–9, 2000, for example, none of the top ten stories covered by ABC, NBC, and CBS, in their early evening newscasts, covered events in other nations. In order of time spent, the top ten included the court trial of the Microsoft Corporation (24 mins. by all of the networks for the week), the opening of a World War II museum in New Orleans (19 mins.), grandparent visitation rights ruling (9 mins.), gas price rises (7 mins.), benefits for gays in

the auto industry (6 mins.), tax vote in Congress (6 mins.), fraud in online auctions (5 mins), airline industry consolidations (5 mins.), health-care reform (5 mins), and crackdowns on illegal Mexican immigration (5 mins.), see *Tyndall Weekly*, 10 June 2000.

38. I discuss this point more fully in *Perspectives on American Political Media* (Boston: Allyn and Bacon, 1997), 152–62.

39. Tucher, 12–31.

40. *Tyndall Special Report*, "Top Stories of 2001."

41. "Public Attentiveness to News Stories: 1986–2000," Pew Center for the People and the Press (online), July 12, 2000; "Terrorism Transforms News Interest; Worries Over New Attacks Decline," Pew Center for the People and Press (online), December 18, 2001.

42. Frank Rich, "The Weight of an Anchor," *New York Times Magazine*, 19 May 2002, 66.

43. For perspectives on how television coverage of politics has changed over the years, see Sig Mickelson, *From Whistle Stop to Sound Bite* (New York: Praeger, 1989), 167–76; and Walter Cronkite, *A Reporter's Life* (New York: Knopf, 1996), 373–84.

44. For example, there appears to be a shrinking audience for election year presidential debates. In 1980 80 million Americans watched Ronald Reagan and Walter Mondale square off in their first debate. The number dropped in 1996 to 46 million, and about the same number in 2000. In the first debate of the 2000 campaign, NBC and Fox did not even carry the debate live, preferring to stay with a baseball playoff game. See Jim Rutenberg, "The 2000 Campaign: the Ratings," *New York Times*, 5 October 2000, A 30.

45. Alison Griffiths, "*Pobol y Cwm*: The Construction of National and Cultural Identity in a Welsh Language Soap Opera" in Drummond, Paterson, and Willis, 9–24.

46. Meyrowitz, 307–11.

47. See, for example, Roderick Hart, *Modern Rhetorical Criticism*, 2d ed. (Boston: Allyn and Bacon, 1997), 184–86.

48. Gary Woodward, "Narrative Form and the Deceptions of Modern Journalism," in *Political Communication Ethics: An Oxymoron?* ed. Robert E. Denton Jr. (Westport, Conn.: Praeger, 2000), 129–39.

49. Joseph Cappella and Kathleen Hall Jamieson, *Spiral of Cynicism: The Press and the Public Good* (New York: Oxford, 1997), 17–37.

50. Bill Carter, "Few Sponsors for TV War News," *New York Times*, 7 February 1991, D1, D20.

51. Neil Postman offers a catalogue of shortcomings in his *Amusing Ourselves to Death* (New York: Viking Penguin, 1985), 83–

113. A more recent summary that also includes print journalism is offered by James Fallows in *Breaking the News: How the Media Undermine American Democracy* (New York: Pantheon, 1996), 129–270.

52. Gitlin, 32.

53. Some writers like Harold Lasswell have tended to pathologize political impulses into a fundamental form of narcissism (*Psychopathology and Politics*, [New York: Viking, 1968], 1–27). Others such as Murray Edelman have catalogued elite-created mystifications hidden in nationalistic appeals (*The Symbolic Uses of Politics*, [Urbana: University of Illinois Press, 1967], 1–43). Both perspectives have merit, but are somewhat limited in their assignments of motive.

54. Robert Hughes, *Culture of Complaint* (New York: Oxford, 1993), 28.

55. Roderick Hart, *Seducing America: How Television Charms the Modern Voter* (New York: Oxford, 1994), 117.

56. Roderick Hart, "Community by Negation," xxvi.

57. Arthur Schlesinger, *The Disuniting of America* (New York: W. W. Norton, 1992), 137.

58. I would argue that believing we have conquered poverty is more illusion than reality, given the high percentage of children in the U.S. who fit the legal definition (about 17 percent). Somini Sengupta, "How Many Poor Children Is Too Many?" *New York Times*, 8 July 2001, sec. 4, p. 3.

59. David Zarefsky, *The Roots of American Community*, a 1995 Carroll Arnold Distinguished Lecture, (Boston: Allyn and Bacon, 1996), 5.

60. See, for example, Robert E. Denton Jr., "Epilogue: Constitutional Authority, Public Morality, and Politics," in *Political Communication Ethics*, 241–42.

61. See, for example, Michael Lind, "The Out of Control Presidency," *The New Republic*, 14 August 1995 (online).

62. This summary is adopted from Murray Smith, "Altered States: Character and Emotional Response in the Cinema," *Cinema Journal*, (Summer 1994): 41. See chapter 3 for an extended discussion of this point.

63. Murray Edelman, *Constructing the Political Spectacle*, (Chicago: University of Chicago Press, 1988), 39.

64. Fred Greenstein, "What the President Means to Americans" in *Choosing the President*, ed. James David Barber (Englewood Cliffs, N.J.: Prentice Hall, 1974), 129–135.

65. Theodore Sorenson, *Kennedy* (New York: Harper and Row, 1965), 11.

66. See, for example, Emmet John Hughes, *The Living Presidency* (New York: Coward, McCann and Geoghegan, 1972), 54–75; Michael Novak, *Choosing Our King* (New York: Macmillan, 1974), 3–53; Arthur M. Schlesinger, Jr., *A Thousand Days* (Boston: Houghton Mifflin, 1965) 77–117.

67. Roderick Hart, Deborah Smith-Howell, and John Llewellyn, "Evolution of Presidential News Coverage," *Political Communication and Persuasion* 7, (1990): 227.

68. David Stockman, *The Triumph of Politics* (New York: Avon, 1987), 9–10.

69. George Stephanopoulos, *All Too Human* (Boston: Little, Brown, 1999), 3

70. One measure of the presidency is its characterization by the late-night talk-show hosts. The detachment and distance reflect in the Letterman and Leno jokes are now tracked as broad indicators of political vulnerability. See, for example, Richard Dunham, "Where Bush is Beating Gore," *Business Week* September 11, 2000, (online).

71. Joe Klein, *The Natural: The Misunderstood Presidency of Bill Clinton* (New York: Doubleday, 2002), 208.

72. Pat Dowell, "Morning Edition," National Public Radio, 8 September 2000 (online transcript, Lexis/Nexis).

73. Quoted in Ibid.

74. A Lexis-Nexis search of articles containing "campaign" and "character" as key terms produced *27* between 1 January and 1 February 1992. For the same period in 2000 *58* articles were found. From 1 January through 1 March 1992, *98* articles were found, as compared with *143* for the same period in 2000. Articles containing "campaign" and "issues" were much more evenly divided over these same of periods: *823* articles for January of 1992, and *996* for January of 2000.

75. Marc Sandalow, "Character Key in First Primary," *San Francisco Chronicle* (online), February 1, 2000.

76. Quoted in Ibid.

77. Putnam, 15–64.; Robert Entman, *Democracy Without Citizens* (New York: Oxford University Press, 1989), 17–29.

78. David Halberstam, preface to Bill Kovach and Tom Rosenstiel, *Warp Speed: America in the Age of Mixed Media* (New York: Century Foundation Press, 1999), iv–x.; Richard Sennett, *The Fall of Public Man* (New York: Vintage, 1974), 1–15; Meyrowitz, 1–15.

79. For a history of political gossip, see Gail Collins, *Scorpion Tongues: The Irresistible History of Gossip in American Politics*

(New York: Harvest Books, 1999). As Collins notes, rumor and gossip have never been absent in American life, but between 1900 and the 1970s the private lives of politicians tended to remain private (9–12).

80. Roderick Hart, "Rhetorical Features of Newcasts about the President," *Critical Studies in Mass Communication* 1, (1984): 260–86.

81. Cronkite, 376.

82. Christopher Lasch's *The Culture of Narcissism* (New York: Warner books, 1979), remains an important argument for the presence of this inward shift.

83. Bellah, et al., 282–83.

84. Putnam, 15–25.

INDEX

A.I.: Artificial Intelligence, 53–54
Adams, Robert, 21
admiring identification, 49, 53
Ahearn, John, 105–12, 118, 162n. 17
Alexie, Sherman, 126, 164n. 16
alignment identification, 50–51, 57–58
All About Eve, 67
allegiance identification, 50, 52–53, 57–58, 138
Allport, Gordon, 37
analogical identification, 30–31, 36
Anniversary Party (The), 67
Anti-Semitism, 72
Aristotle, 5–9, 25, 105
Arlen, Michael, 156n. 51
Ashe, Arthur, 66, 157n. 59
associative identification, 2–3, 49–50, 56
audiences, 6, 9, 13, 16, 101–5, 118–19
Augustine, 18

Balazs, Bela, 46, 154n. 2
Barrett, Harold, 97
Barry, Philip, 71
Beatty, Warren, 101, 117, 162n. 12
Beecher, Henry Ward, 63
Bellah, Robert, 17–18, 123, 144, 153n. 58
Belton, John, 156n. 38
Beschloss, Michael, 160n. 49
Blum, W. C., 24

Boorstin, Daniel, 156n. 47
Booth, Wayne, 45, 154n. 4
Bordwell, David, 154n. 4
Brock, Bernard, 22, 26, 160n. 6, 151n. 21
Brown, Jesse, 88
Buffalo Bill Cody, 63
Bulworth, 100–5, 117
Burke, Kenneth, ix, 1, 4–6, 8, 13, 15, 18, 21–33, 42–43, 45, 92, 98, 137, 145, 151n. 27, 152n. 37, 152n. 43, 153n. 52
    definition of man, 11, 23–24
    perspectives on identification 21–33
    varieties of identification, 26, 29–32
Bush, George H. W., 85, 89, 139
Bush, George W., 89, 94, 139, 141

Calamity Jane, 49
Cable News Network, 135
Cameron, James, 54
campaigns (political), 35–36, 85, 97–98, 101, 166n. 44, 168n. 70, 168n. 74
Canadian identity, 121–23, 130–31, 144
Cantwell, Mary, 121
Cappella, Joseph, 166n. 49
Caro, Robert, 158n. 13
Cash, Johnny, 9
cathartic identification, 49
Celebrity, 67

171

celebrity, 13–15, 47, 61–69
   cultural effects of, 63–69
   cycles of, 67–69
   disclosure of character and,
      64–65, 67, 69
   privacy and, 66–67
Challenger (Space Shuttle),
   128–29, 133
Chaplin, Charlie, 50, 61, 100
Charland, Maurice, 163n. 4
Cheney, George, 152n. 34
Chesebro, James, 150n. 6
Cicero, 25
civic engagement. See identification:
   civil life
Civil Action (A) (Harr), 17
civil rights, 75–84
Clayman, Steven, 161n. 6
Clinton, Bill, 17, 28–29, 65, 71,
   74, 83–95, 100, 138–39, 141
   influences on, 83–85, 169n. 35
   relations with military, 86–87
Coast Guard, 115–16
Cohen, Mitchell, 159n. 33
Collins, Gail, 168n. 79
Coming Into the Country (McPhee),
   73
commonplaces, 6–8, 89
communication, 5, 10–11, 13, 18,
   22, 24–25
consciousness, xi, 24, 26–27
consubstantiality, 8–9
Cooper, Brenda, 155n. 24
Copland, Aaron, x, 3–4, 45, 72,
   157n. 2
counter cinema, 54–55
Counter-Statement (Burke), 24
Cox, Brian, 73
credibility, 138–43
Cronkite, Walter, 166n. 43
C-SPAN, 102
Cukor, George, 71
culture wars, 32–33, 122
Cynics of Greece, 99, 102

Dallek, Robert, 77
Day, Dennis G., 151n. 18

Day, Doris, 48–49, 72
DeLay, Tom, 94
Denton, Robert, 167n. 60
Diamond, Elin, 1
Dideon, Joan, 61–62
Dillard, Annie, 6
Dionne, E. J., 152n. 31
Distefano, Lisa, 116
Duncan, Hugh, D., 16, 22, 57
Dunham, Richard, 168n. 70
Dunne, John Gregory, 61–62
Dyer, Richard, 156n. 46

Edelman, Murray, 139, 167n. 53
Eisenberg, Evan, 4
Eisenhower, Dwight, 142
Ensler, Eve, 73
enthymemes, 7–8
Entman, Robert, 165n. 27
Erikson, Patricia, 115

Fallows, James, 167n. 51
Feilitzen, Cecilia, 154n. 12
Festinger, Leon, 153n. 54
Film. See narrative, film theory,
   and point of view
film theory, xi, 41, 47–48, 54
Finn, Robin, 157n. 60
Fisher, Matthew, 130
Frankel, Max, 69
Freud, Sigmund, ix, 13–14, 18, 21,
   26, 47
Fulbright, J. William, 84

Gabler, Neil, 72, 158n. 3
Gaonkar, Dilip, 149n. 36, 150n. 3
Gergen, David, 93
Giddons, Elizabeth, 73, 158n. 6
Gingrich, Newt, 85, 94
Gitlin, Todd, 121, 136, 155n. 32
Goddard, Paulette, 51
Goffman, Erving, 15, 39
Goldman, William, 61
Goldwater, Barry, 97
Goodwin, Doris, 157n. 61
Goodwin, Richard, 80
Gorgias (Plato), 9–10

Gorgias, 9
Grant, Cary, 13
Gresson, Aaron D., III, 148n. 11
group identification, 9, 112–19,
    121–27, 135–38
Guthrie, W. K. C., 10

Halberstam, David, 142
Handel, George Frederick, 124
Harr, Jonathan, 17
Harris, Wendell, 39
Hart, Rod, 123, 137, 140, 164n.
    11, 166n. 47, 167n. 55, 168n.
    67, 169n. 80
Hayworth, Rita, 48
Hepburn, Katharine, 71
Herder, J. G., 123
Hitchcock, Alfred, 58–60
Hoffman, Abbie, 99
hooks, bell, 126, 164n. 16
Horton, Donald, 62, 156n. 44
Hughes, Robert, 33, 136–37, 162n.
    11
Hunter, James Davison, 152n. 48

identification:
    adaptation as, 24–27, 71–92
    alignment, 50–51, 57–58
    allegiance and, 50, 52–53,
        57–58, 138
    analogical, 30–31, 36
    assimilation as, 5, 72
    civil life and, 18, 63–65, 94–95,
        101, 121–35, 143–45
    commonplaces and, 6–7, 89
    consciousness and, 26–27, 41
    consubstantiality and, 8–9
    defined, ix–x, 1–2, 4–5, 18, 138
    demographic verses ideological, x
    failed, 16, 54, 93–95, 97–119,
        138–43
    film and, 41, 45–69, 72
    form and, 4, 24
    identity adjustment and, 33–39
    ideological, 31–33, 36
    limits of models, 26–27, 39–41
    logical structure of, 7–8

mechanical, 29–30
music and, 2–4, 42, 72, 99, 124
opposite of division, 15, 26–29
pandering and, 9–10, 101
point of view and, 48, 57–61
psychological versus rhetorical,
    ix
representational art and, 3,
    105–12
rhetorical perspective on, 5–12,
    27–28, 41–42, 118–19, 145
roll-taking and, 13–17, 101–4
sympathetic, 49, 53, 67
See also communication, public
    opinion, and identity
identity, 13–15, 32–39, 48, 112–19:
    Canadian, 121–23, 130–31, 144
    national, 17–18, 121–35
    news and, 131–35
    sub-national, 9, 112–19, 121–27,
        135–38
ideographs, 129–31
ideological identification, x,
    31–33, 36
Ignatieff, Michael, 125
Il Postino, 45
International Whaling Commission,
    114
Internationale, 99
Interpretation of Dreams (The),
    (Freud) 13–14

Jameson, Frederic, 130
Jamieson, Kathleen Hall, 166n. 49
Japanese identification, 9
Jauss, Hans, 49–50, 54, 56
Johnson, Ken, 162n. 17
Johnson, Lyndon, 28, 71, 74–83,
    89, 92–94, 158n. 16, 160n. 49:
    experiences as teacher, 82
    voting rights speech to joint
        session of Congress, 75–82
Jourdain, Robert, 3

Kael, Pauline, 155n. 30
Kandel, Eric, 147n. 1
Kelly, Grace, 58

Kennedy, George, 148n. 19
Kennedy, John F., 12, 28, 64, 69, 74, 82, 128, 139–42
Kennedy, Robert, 64, 82, 84
King Lear (Shakespeare), 73
King, Larry, 85
King, Martin Luther, 64, 75–76, 81, 84, 109, 128
Klein, Joe, 71, 140–41
Korda, Michael, 51
Kramer, Jane, 106, 109, 112

Lasch, Christopher, 39, 156n. 54, 189n. 82
Lasswell, Harold, 167n. 53
Lentricchia, Frank, 150n. 1
Lexis-Nexis, 168n. 74
Lin, Maya, 106
Lincoln, Abraham, 92
Linne, Olga, 154n. 12
Lipset, Seymour Martin, 125
Llewellyn, John, 168n. 67
Lonergan, Kenneth, 56

MacLeish, Archibald, 40–41
Makah Tribe, 100, 112–19
Malcolm X, 64, 109
Mamet, David, 8, 153n. 59
Manhattan Memoir (Cantwell), 121
Maraniss, David, 159n. 32
Marshall, P. David, 49–50, 53–54, 56, 67–68
Marx Brothers, 105
Marx, Karl, 21, 26
Maslow, Abraham, 153n. 60
Mazzella, Anthony, 154n. 8
McCarty, Micah, 113, 115
McGee, Michael, 129, 165n. 29
McLuhan, Marshall, 127, 164n. 15
McPhee, John, 73
Mead, George Herbert, 12–13, 16, 18, 21
mechanical identification, 29–30
Meech Lake Accord, 122
Memorial Day Speech (Clinton), 28–29, 87–95

memory, 1–3
Menand, Louis, 97
Messiah (Handel), 124
Metz, Christian, 154n. 5
Meyrowitz, Joshua, 39, 66, 124, 134, 142, 157n. 62
Mickelson, Sig, 166n. 43
Midnight Cowboy, 56
misidentification, 97–119
Modern Dogma and the Rhetoric of Assent (Booth), 45
Modern Times, 51
Modleski, Tania, 156n. 37
Monaco, James, 155n. 27
Monroe, Marilyn, 66, 157n. 59
Mormon Church, 126–27
Mulvey, Laura, 58, 156n. 37
Murrow, Edward R., 40, 66

NAACP, 97–98
Nark, Janis, 88
narrative, 6, 16–17, 34–35, 39, 41–43, 45–69, 72, 100, 128–29, 141–42:
commercial versus independent, 54–56
postmodern, 54–55
Nash, Alanna, 62
National Endowment for the Arts, 33
Natural (The) (Klein), 71
Newcomb, Horace, 165n. 36
New Left, 65, 84, 159n. 33
Nichols, Marie H., 22
Nixon, 141
Nixon, Richard, 66, 89
Nussbaum, Martha, 123

Oliver, Robert, 25, 151n. 19
On Moonlight Bay, 72
Oravec, Christine, 29–32
other-direction, 37–39, 92–95

Painter, Nell, 68–69
parasocial interaction, 62
Pattison, Sheron Daily, 151n. 10

Pearl Harbor, 51–52
Perelman, Chaim, 4
Perot, Ross, 97–98, 100
Persian Gulf War, 135
Persico, Joseph, 160n. 40
Person to Person, 66
persuasion. *See* identification,
    audiences, and communication
Pew Research Center, 133
Philadelphia Story (The), 71
Pikser, Jeremy, 162n. 12
Plato, 9–11
Platt, Oliver, 102
point of view, 48, 57–61
Pollack, Howard, 157n. 2
Popper, Karl, 149n. 34
Postman, Neil, 166n. 51
post-modern narrative, 54–55
Powell, Colin, 86, 88, 90, 160n. 40
*Presentation of Self in Everyday
    Life (The)* (Goffman), 15–16
presidency, 16, 65, 69, 74–95,
    138–43, 158n. 9, 166n. 44
Pretty Woman, 55–56
Prokofiev, Serge, 2
Protagoras, 11
*Psychology of Persuasive Speech
    (The)* (Oliver), 25
public opinion, 10–11, 77, 87, 92,
    95, 110, 133
Putnam, Robert, 126, 144, 164n. 17

Quayle, Dan, 99–100
Quintilian, 25

racism, 75–83, 102–5, 109
Raubicheck, Walter, 154n. 8
Raymond and Toby (Ahearn),
    107–9
Reagan, Ronald, 16, 128–29, 140,
    159n. 37
Rear Window, 58–60
Reischauer, Edwin, 9
Rhetoric, (Aristotle) 5–6
Rhetoric of Motives (A), (Burke) 1,
    21, 29

Richard, Maurice, 130
Riesman, David, 37–39
Roberts, Julia, 56, 61
Rockwell, Norman, 72
roll-taking as identification, 13–17,
    101–4
Roosevelt, Eleanor, 69, 73
Roosevelt, Franklin, 69, 73, 89,
    142
Roosevelt, Theodore, 89
Rubin, Jerry, 99
Rueckert, William, 22, 27, 150n. 2,
    151n. 25
Run Lola Run, 60–61
Russell, Richard, 74–75
Rutenberg, Jim, 166n. 44

Sarup, Madan, 34
Savitch, Jessica, 62
sculpture, 105–12
Sea Shepherd Society, 115
Segal, George, 106, 162n. 13
Selma, Alabama, 76–77, 81, 83
Senate (U.S.), 74–75, 84
Sengupta, Somini, 167n. 58
Sennett, Richard, 63, 142
Seventh Symphony (Shostakovich),
    99
Shakespeare, William, 73, 100
Shostakovich, Dmitri, 99
Simons, Herbert, 149n. 35,
    150n. 3
Smith, Anthony, 164n. 10
Smith, Murray, 50–52, 56, 67–68,
    167n. 62
Smith-Howell, Deborah, 168n. 67
Sophists, 9–11, 23
Sorensen, Ted, 139
Spielberg, Steven, 53
Squire, Larry, 147n. 1
Srebnick, Walter, 154n. 8
Stacey, Jackie, 48
Stella, Joseph, 3, 147n. 4
Stephanopoulos, George, 140
Stewart, Jimmy, 58
Stockman, David, 140

Strauss, Anselm, 13
Stuckey, Mary, 165n. 25
Sullivan, Robert, 117–18, 162n. 25
sympathetic identification, 49, 53, 67

Tarkington, Booth, 72
terrorism, 17, 133, 135
Thelma and Louise, 52
Theory of the Leisure Class (Veblen), 30
Thompson, Richard, 147n. 2
Time magazine, 140
Titanic, 49, 54–55
Torres, Rigoberto, 106
Traffic, 55
transcendence (verbal), x, 27–29
Tribe, Laurence, 29
Troisi, Massimo, 45
Trudeau, Pierre, 130, 163n. 5
Truman, Harry, 159n. 19
Truth, Sojourner, 69
Tucher, Andie, 164n. 20
Twilight of Common Dreams (The) (Gitlin), 121
Tykwer, Tom, 60
Tyndall Weekly, 166n. 37
Tyndall Special Report, 166n. 40

Underwood, Doug, 164n. 19
United Negro College Fund, 99
Up Close and Personal, 62

Vagina Monologues (The) (Ensler), 73
Veblen, Thorstein, 21, 30, 32
Vidal, Gore, 162n. 11
Vietnam POWs, 91
Vietnam Veterans Memorial, 87–88, 106
Vietnam War, 28, 34, 77, 84
Voting Rights Act of 1965, 74–83

Wainwright, Heather, 110, 162n. 22
Wallace, George, 71
Warner Brothers, 72
Warner, W. Lloyd, 129, 165n. 28
Watson, Paul, 115
Wayne, John, 14–15, 61
Webster, Daniel, 12
whaling, 112–19
Wild West Show, 63
Wills, Garry, 15
Winans, James, 25, 151n. 18
Windt, Ted, 99, 171n. 9
Wohl, R. Richard, 62, 156n. 44
Wollen, Peter, 54
Wright, Mark, 150n. 1

You Can Count on Me, 56

Zarefsky, David, 137–38, 167n. 59